LONDON TROLLEYBUS CHRONOLOGY 1931-1962

Front cover:
The inspectors' hut at Plaistow sets the scene as the driver is about to board
'L3' class No 1455, to take it on to Chingford Mount. The 'L3s' were AEC/MCCW
chassisless vehicles.

Rear cover, top:
Between November 1941 and June 1943, 43 trolleybuses destined for export to
South Africa were diverted to London Transport. Eighteen were AECs and the
remainder Leylands, and all had bodywork by MCCW. Here we see an
unidentified Leyland on route 693, about to depart for Chadwell Heath.

Rear cover, bottom:
Camden Lock Bridge is the setting for 'N1' No 1574 on route 639. The 'N1s'
were AECs with BRCW bodies.

Overleaf:
Stage thirteen on 2 January 1962 saw the end of operations at Colindale,
Finchley and Stonebridge depots and routes 645, 660, 662 & 666. This splendid
view, taken in August 1959, shows 'N1' No 1617 turning at the Jubilee Clock,
Harlesden. The 'N1' and 'N2' classes, along with some 'L3s', worked these routes
at the end after moving across from the East End of London. *London Transport*

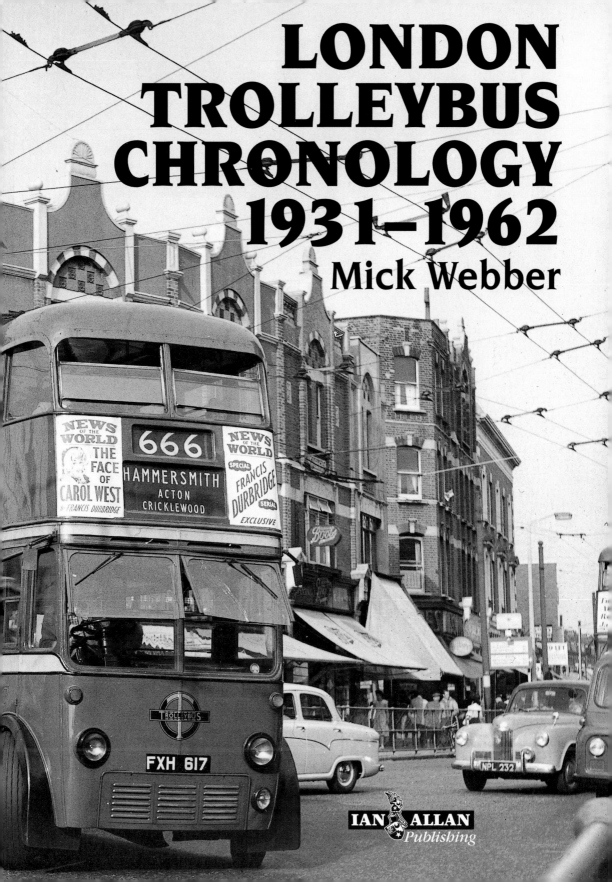

LONDON TROLLEYBUS CHRONOLOGY 1931–1962

Mick Webber

Ian ALLAN Publishing

CONTENTS

Below:
'N1' brothers Nos 1611 and 1576 at Paddenswick Road, Hammersmith. Late running buses towards Hammersmith turned short here, originally on batteries, but it was wired up in November 1955. It did, however, require a pole swap, hence the bamboo pole hanging on the traction standard.

Bottom:
In July 1960 Hammersmith closed to operations and became a BEA coach base. Its routes 626, 628 and 630 were withdrawn. Typical of its stock was this 'D2' No 422 on the 626 at Clapham Junction on a fine sunny afternoon.
Norman Rayfield,
LCC Tramways Trust

First published 1997

ISBN 0 7110 2528 2

Published by Ian Allan Publishing

an imprint of Ian Allan Ltd, Terminal House, Station Approach, Shepperton, Surrey TW17 8AS.
Printed by Ian Allan Printing Ltd at its works at Coombelands in Runnymede, England.

Code: 9707/B2

Picture credit
All pictures uncredited are from the author's collection.

It would be easy to understand how the Londoner of the 1930s would be impressed by the new trolleybus. To say that its ride qualities were superior to those of the tramcar would be an understatement; the silent smooth operation, and bright and comfortable interiors, must indeed have been a revelation. Of the 50 trolleybus systems to operate in the British Isles, London was one of 18 to adopt this form of transport in the 1930s, and eventually was to dwarf all others, with 1,891 vehicles being built. (Wolverhampton, with 354, was the next down the ladder.)

Despite the fact that the system has now been defunct for more years than it actually existed, its popularity is still considerable. It wasn't just the vehicles of course that roused interest. It was a whole way of life, just like the

INTRODUCTION

trams before them. There was the overhead and complex junctions to marvel at, crossovers and points, and the anticipation of a possible dewirement when you knew that the driver was going too fast, or turning too sharply on a bend. The trolleybus driver's job was a very skilful one and considerably more complex than most passengers behind him would have believed. His task on the new RT or Routemaster bus would be a lot easier. The tower wagons and crews, and the busy breakdown tenders on their way to change a wheel or mend a trolley boom, all these things combined to make a fascinating subject, and of course, a good excuse for a book.

Above:
'D3' No 529 turns into Tamworth Road, Croydon, on route 630. This Hammersmith vehicle is showing a set of Charlton-made blinds, on what was London's second longest trolleybus route. *G. E. Baddeley*

Left:
'E2' No 607 waits at North Woolwich terminus on route 669 on 20 November 1959. The extension to North Woolwich was previously unserved by trams. *Brian Speller*

Most other publications seem to refer to the trolleybus as a 'curious hybrid', but I would disagree; it was always the natural progression from the tramcar, and was an effective form of public transport in its own right. Unfortunately, in the 1950s and 1960s money to renew ageing infrastructure was not readily available and it was all too easy to announce abandonment rather than renewal. Certainly pollution wasn't the issue that it is today, and therefore the financial argument was the only one that carried any weight.

My own personal memories flood back every time I look through photographs, and many are still vivid in my mind. The ride with Mum, when I was about eight, on a 696 from Woolwich to Welling, impressed me greatly. It was my first, and the acceleration of the vehicle quite amazed me. How was it that this bus didn't make any noise — well, not the noise I was used to — and no smoke from the back?

That certain sound through the wires when

a trolleybus was approaching is difficult to put into words. The drumming noise through the roof when the trolley heads went over a junction, I can still hear it now. The diesel bus could never match it for acceleration and vibration-free travel. I remember well the bitter

Below:
A dull, drizzly day at Highgate Village, and Nos 1052 and 1358 stand over on route 611, both vehicles being fitted with coasting and runback brakes for Highgate Hill. *Brian Speller*

Opposite above:
West Ham church and chassisless 'L3' vehicles Nos 1498 and 1396 pass, working on West Ham depot's circular service 690. The route worked a loop at East Ham, the 689 operating in the opposite direction. *David Packer*

Opposite below:
No 993B had been rebodied by East Lancs in December 1947, after war damage in 1944, and is seen here at North Finchley about to work short to Finsbury Park on route 521. *Michael Rooum*

disappointment shared with my friend Pete, when we arrived at Shoreditch to photograph trolleybuses in the area. We saw the wires but only new Routemasters, the conversion having occurred earlier that week, instead of the following week, as we had believed. Not to be denied, we travelled on to Wood Green, and later Colindale, where I paid my first visit to the scrapyard, emerging with an AEC wheel hub. It just fitted into my bag and carrying it around all day nearly dislocated my shoulder.

Funnily enough, one of the most vivid memories to me is the time when I jumped on a 660 at Golders Green, for the trip to Hammersmith. It started to rain heavily, and when we reached Acton Market Place, the conductor announced that we would be turning short at Bromyard Avenue. When we stopped, and all of the steaming wet coats had gone, I remained on the upper deck, wiping the condensation from the front windows. Sitting alone, I listened to the wipers struggling back and forth downstairs, while the driver and conductor chatted on the platform below, their words drifting up the stairs. I was determined not to get soaked waiting for another, so I stayed on. On the

journey back, people came and went, leaving puddles on the floor, the water slowly running along the ticket-filled gutter to the partly blocked drain holes. The lights were on all the way back to Cricklewood, where I got soaked waiting for a 16 to Victoria. I will also always remember the driver at Stonebridge Park, who chatted to me when taking a meal break. He took my name and address, saying, 'I'll send you my cap badge when this is all over.' He did too, and if he reads this, I thank him sincerely.

The format of this book is that of a diary of

Above:
Claremont Road, Surbiton, on 31 March 1962. Just five weeks to go before the scene was to change for ever, 'L3s' Nos 1499 and 1526 are about to pass each other on route 601.

Opposite above:
No 1822 was from the first batch of 'Q1s' and was delivered in July 1948. These vehicles operated at first only from Fulwell and Isleworth depots, but from 1953 they began to appear on the 607 from Hanwell.

Opposite below:
'C3' class No 343 carried bodywork by the Birmingham Railway Carriage and Wagon Co and was delivered in August 1936. It is seen here at Acton Vale on route 666.

events as they happened, from the takeover by London Transport in 1933, showing the shaping of the fleet and network, taking us through the war, into the peace, and on to the eventual demise. I have not attempted to chronicle route histories, or detail wiring layouts, as these have been dealt with admirably elsewhere in other recent publications. Therefore route commencement dates are shown but not all subsequent alterations.

I have collected the facts together and presented them in a new and hopefully enlightening way, drawing on information from many sources. Apart from the vehicles themselves, the service fleet and depots are also dealt with in separate chapters. As usual with this type of book, photographs are the

key and I have tried to present the best cross-section to illustrate the story, and have endeavoured to select previously unpublished material wherever possible. Where it has been possible to credit the source, I have done so, but some pictures have proved impossible to attribute, and any photographers uncredited must please accept my sincere apologies.

Many people have helped with this task including Ron Harrington, formerly with George Cohen, Ian Gibson of Lancashire Museums and Rosalind Thistlewood, who both helped with the Leyland archive material. I would also like to thank Peter Horner and Robin Newell, who helped and encouraged me during the work on this book, and John

Shearman who drew up the information in the appendices.

If you want to see and ride on a London Trolleybus again, then go to the East Anglia Transport Museum near Lowestoft, where you can turn the clock back once more. They have Nos 260 and 1521 resident there, with visits from No 1768. No 1348 resides in Dublin and No 796 in Paris, while Nos 1201 and 1812, home from Spain, await restoration at Sandtoft. The London Transport Museum owns Nos 1 and 1253.

As trams make a comeback in many towns, it is hard to understand why the trolleybus has not joined it on the drawing board. Whether it will ever return to London is doubtful, but whatever happens, it will remain an important part of London's transport history, completing nearly 31 years of operation. I hope you enjoy this ride through London's trolleybus history as much as I enjoyed putting it all together, and I dedicate it to my long-suffering wife, Coral.

Below:
'N1' No 1627 was a wartime delivery in February 1940, also with bodywork by BRCW. The terminus for the northern end of Bow's route 661 was Lea Bridge depot, where it is here pictured.

**Mick Webber
Blackheath, March 1997**

When the London Passenger Transport Board took on the awesome task of integrating the capital's transport systems on 1 July 1933, it inherited a vast array of vehicles and operators, and an area that generally stretched to a radius of 30 miles from Charing Cross. Apart from the London General Omnibus Co and numerous private motorbus fleets, it acquired the tramways of the London County Council, London United, Metropolitan Electric and South Metropolitan, as well as all of the local authority systems, and the Underground railway network. Lord Ashfield, Frank Pick and the other members of the Board would have their work cut out getting to grips with all of that, but there was food for thought, because with the acquisition of the London United Tramways came that undertaking's fleet of 61 trolleybuses.

CHAPTER 1
IN THE
BEGINNING

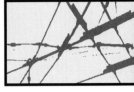

The LUT had decided in 1930 to apply for powers to replace any part of its tramway network with trolleybuses, which it felt would be far more economic on its less busy routes. These powers were approved on 1 August of that year and by October the LUT had wired up the Teddington to Twickenham section. An AEC/English Electric demonstrator was hired for trials and, following its success, an order for 60 vehicles was placed, the first of which was delivered in February 1931 amid much public interest. By May, enough had been received for the company to commence operations between these two points and it went ahead on the 16th. The vehicles were based on AEC 663T chassis, and carried half-cab bodywork by the Union Construction and Finance Co, which had previously built the Feltham trams. They featured English Electric equipment in the case of Nos 1-35, and British Thomson Houston on Nos 36-60. By June, the route had reached Kingston, and by September Wimbledon was served and all of the local Kingston services had been converted.

A vehicle that could pull in to the kerb to pick up passengers and overtake other traffic was always going to be a winner with the public and crews alike, and the trolleybus was an instant success. The initial savings were impressive: 15% less cost per mile than the

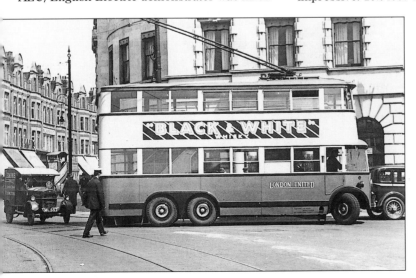

Left:
With bodies by the Union Construction & Finance Co and AEC chassis, London United Tramways had a fleet of 60 such vehicles, which were inherited by the LTPB in 1933. They dated from 1931, and No 2 is seen here turning at Twickenham.

looking three-axle trolleybus, with a full front, centre entrance with folding doors, and taking full advantage of the newly permitted 30ft length. LUT received the new vehicle on 20 March 1933 but, alas, only had just over three months to evaluate its potential before the London Passenger Transport Board took over. During June 1933 this vehicle was demonstrated in Bournemouth to the Electrical Convention.

Very early on, the Board, like many other operators before it, decided that the legacy of the tram, the infrastructure, was too big an investment to waste, and saw the trolleybus as the obvious replacement for the tramways it had inherited. Based on the success LUT had enjoyed, it soon announced that it intended to replace the whole tramway system with trolleybuses. In 1934 it sought powers from Parliament to begin the task, starting with 90 route miles which included the rest of the former LUT services, the South Metropolitan section, the former operations of Dartford, Bexley and Erith Councils, and part of the Metropolitan. They were so confident of approval that in March 1934 they ordered two new vehicles as possible prototypes for the fleet that was to be built. The two were to be numbered 62 and 63. No 62 was based on the six-wheel AEC 663T chassis, with traditional rear open platform, 73-seater bodywork by Metro-Cammell and electrical equipment by Metrovick. It was delivered in July 1934. No 63 followed in August and had a two-axle AEC 661T chassis, with English Electric supplying the electrical equipment and building the 60-seater bodywork.

Both vehicles had half-width bulkheads. They were allocated to Fulwell depot for evaluation purposes, where they were operated mainly on route 4. The powers sought were granted as expected in July 1934 and, as a further step towards the future, provision was made in the bus route renumbering scheme of October 1934 for trolleybus services to use the 500 and 600 series of numbers.

After thorough testing, the Board eventually decided that the six-wheeler was more suitable for the task, the seating capacity's comparability with that of the tram being the

trams; more passenger miles — LUT was on to a winner. Profits were increasing and, in 1932, the company applied for an extension at Tolworth, beyond the former tram terminus, to the bypass. This was approved and work started, although it did not come into being in LUT's lifetime.

Flushed with success, LUT was now keen to experiment and find a vehicle suitable for more heavily used routes, one which could match the seating capacity of the tram. Much thought was given to the new vehicle; AEC provided the 691T chassis, the only one ever made, English Electric the motor and the body was built by the London General Omnibus Co at Chiswick. The result was a very modern-

Above:
The other trolleybus to be taken over by the Board was No 61, the experimental centre-entrance bus with an LGOC body. In June 1933, just one month before the takeover, it was demonstrated to the Electrical Convention at Bournemouth.

Opposite above:
The Board's first prototype six-wheeler was No 62, delivered in July 1934. It was an AEC with MCCW bodywork, and the basic forerunner of the huge fleet that followed. It is seen here in latter days at Aldgate. The rear offside lower deck window was later panelled over. It was unique in that it had more interior lights than any other London trolleybus.

Opposite below:
The other prototype, which was to remain unique, was the four-wheeled No 63. This was also an AEC but with bodywork by English Electric. It was tried alongside No 62 after its delivery in August 1934 but came off second best. During the run-up to operations at Bexley, late in 1935, it made an appearance at the depot and was tried on some sections of route prior to opening. The date is 5 August 1935.

major factor. Plans were drawn up for the alteration and rebuilding that would be needed to make tram depots suitable for trolleybus operation. Having made this decision, the Board published in 1935 its 'Form for tender and specification for a double-deck trolleybus'. This publication spelt out first the terms of tender to the prospective supplier, followed by a very exacting specification for the chassis, electrical equipment and bodywork. It concluded with a form on which the manufacturers could enter their price for the work, according to the quantity ordered. The booklet was sent out, together with the official drawings. It stated that the vehicle should not exceed 13 tons in the event of a 70-seater and 12¼ tons for a 60-seater, and that it 'should be silent at all loads and speeds up to and including 38mph, and the bodywork free from drumming.' Wiring was specified to be 550V, with provision for 32 and 28 12W bulbs in the 70- and 60-seaters respectively, although this was not adhered to. Windows, when closed, should be leakproof when subjected to water pressure up to 300psi, and 5% of each vehicle type were to be tilt tested by the Ministry of Transport at the supplier's cost. Where necessary, all removable parts should be stamped 'LPTB'. Item 49 of the bodywork section is particularly interesting, as it states, 'The front and rear boxes shall be fitted with a glass transparency bearing the word Trolleybus, which shall be illuminated by two electric lamps'. This item was later deleted.

Orders were placed in February 1935 for 120 vehicles, which it was hoped would be delivered in time to convert the first routes before the end of the year.

Leyland was to supply 68 short-wheelbase TTB2 chassis with Metrovick electrical equipment and the order for the bodywork was shared. Nos 64-93 were classified 'B1' and were built by the Birmingham Railway Carriage and Wagon Co, and Nos 94-131, class 'B2', came from Brush Electrical Engineering.

All had seats for 60, and featured half-width bulkheads.

The two types were very similar but the 'B1s' had a nearside fixed windscreen, whereas the 'B2s' had two openers. The 'B2s' had a square window opener in the cab door, where the 'B1s' had a sloping one. They were all delivered with the small staircase window, as on the 'C1s', although many were later panelled over. The 'B1s' were fitted with coasting and runback brakes for use on the Anerley Hill section of the South Metropolitan route; these restricted the vehicle speed in either forward or backward direction in the event of a failure.

AEC was to build 52 on its 664T chassis, which would have English Electric electrical equipment.

The order for the bodywork was split between Weymann, which would build Nos 132-141, and Metro-Cammell, which supplied Nos 142-183. All had half-width bulkheads and seats for 70, and were classified 'C1'. As a different bodybuilder usually caused the Board to create a trolleybus class distinction, it is surprising that the MCCW batch did not become 'C2', to distinguish them from the Weymann 'C1s'.

No 183 differed from the rest, as it was fitted with rear wheel 'spats', which featured later on 'C2' and 'C3' vehicles. All of the 'C1s' were built with a small window high up on the rear offside, to give light to the staircase. They also had small side lights set in the cream band

14

between decks and the only point of distinction between the two products was the positioning of these, the Weymann versions having them set slightly lower than those on the Metro-Cammell counterparts.

With these 120 vehicles due later that year, the Board realised that there was a need to place further orders if it was to maintain the rate of conversions into 1936, and therefore another order

was placed for a further 300 trolleybuses: 200 from AEC and 100 from Leyland.

The idea of operating trolleybuses in Alexandra Park had been discussed for some months but the whole plan was dropped in the summer of 1935 as the subsidy offered by the Trustees was considered insufficient, thus denying Londoners possibly the most scenic route on the system, and interesting in that the low railway bridges along the route precluded the use of double-deckers. Another Bill was placed before Parliament for powers to operate over more MET territory, and for the first time into the East End and the former East and West Ham, Ilford, Barking, Leyton and Walthamstow systems. This was duly passed

Opposite:
Being delivered at the same time as the 'B' classes were the 'C' class vehicles. The 'C1s' were AECs with MCCW bodies and were 30ft 70-seaters. They were originally allocated to Fulwell and Hounslow for routes 667 and 657. No 160 is shown here on the 657.

Top:
No 180, also a 'C1', is waiting on the stand at Hammersmith on route 667, ready for the trip to Hampton Court. There will not be many day trippers, however, as this is late in the year, 1935, the vehicle having been delivered in October. *Ian Allan Library*

Above:
The Brush factory at Loughborough was busy in the latter months of 1935, turning out the 'B2' class buses. The 'B' classes were the first Leylands to join the fleet and were all short wheelbase 60-seaters. No 94 is seen here at the factory, one of 21 delivered in October 1935. *Brush of Loughborough, courtesy Leicestershire Record Office*

registered TJ 9010. Its spell with London Transport does not appear to be well documented and no information has come to light of its demonstration.

Decision on the standardisation of current collection was made at about this time and the trolley wheel favoured by the LUT was abandoned in favour of skids with carbon inserts, which were quieter and much less prone to dewirement.

Back to new deliveries, and the first of the order for 120 appeared at Fulwell on 5 October, when Leyland 'B1' No 94, and AEC 'C1' No 142 bounced over the cobblestones. In all, 21 'B1s' and 47 'C1s' were taken into stock during October, enough for the Board to commence its first conversion, finishing off what LUT had started by eliminating the trams from the last Fulwell route between Hampton Court and Hammersmith, and changing over completely at Hounslow on its only route from Shepherds Bush to Hounslow. These routes, numbered 667 and 657 respectively, came into being on 27 October and for this Hounslow depot had been extensively rebuilt and a traverser and turntable installed.

With the beginning of London Transport trolleybus operation, a change in the spacing between the running wires was implemented and the LUT standard of 18in was changed to 24in. Power substations were provided at approximately 2-mile intervals.

November saw another 33 Leyland 'B1s' and 'B2s' roll in from the factories and a further four 'C1s' from Southall. This was sufficient to begin the next phase, which the Board was anxious to carry out in the southeast at Bexleyheath, where the tram tracks in the surrounding area were in particularly bad condition. Here a completely new depot for the trolleybuses had been built; the first and only time an existing tram depot site was not utilised. The Erith and Bexley UDC depots did

on 10 July and a further 59 route miles were authorised. A further Act of Parliament of note was passed on 2 August, allowing Government financial support for the new works programme of 1935-40. It was mainly to finance the expanding Underground system, but included in the overall low-interest loan was a sum of £5.2 million for new trolleybuses.

Another interesting event during the year was the use of a Leyland demonstrator. The unique, and so to remain, Leyland Low Floor trolleybus had been exhibited at the 1935 Olympia Commercial Motor Show. It had 63-seat Massey dual entrance bodywork and was

not meet the Board's requirements and were not taken into ownership.

'B2' class Leylands were put into store at Bexley, pending the start of new route 698 from Woolwich Free Ferry to Bexleyheath via Erith, which commenced on 10 November, and on the 24th of that month route 696 followed, running between Woolwich Free Ferry and Dartford via Welling. This then was the end for the former Bexley, Erith and Dartford UDC systems, although the link with the trams was to remain between Abbey Wood and Woolwich, where the wires were to be shared between Free Ferry and Bostall Hill until the end of the trams in July 1952. It should be mentioned here that a few 'C1s' did operate from Bexley at this time, albeit briefly, as did some 'B' class vehicles from Fulwell and Hounslow. A point of interest regarding Bexley depot is that it featured a complete loop wired around the building, which could serve as a test track or training circuit. This was one of only two on the system, the other being at Stonebridge Park.

During December six more 'B' class Leylands were taken into stock and there were now enough new vehicles to move the changeover programme south to Sutton tram depot. The contractor Clough Smith had been at work on the wiring between Sutton and West Croydon, the old South Metropolitan depot had been completely rebuilt and 'B1s' were drafted in to replace the trams on new route 654, which commenced on 8 December between the two points mentioned. At Sutton the route was extended a quarter of a mile beyond the former tram terminus, where a turning loop could be built at Sutton Green. This section was provided with silver-painted fluted traction standards, in accordance with the local council's wishes for something more ornate. To make up for vehicle shortages during the first weeks, three of the LUT Diddlers were borrowed from Fulwell. The last act of the year was to top up the order book by placing a further 170 trolleybuses on order for the new year.

So, as the Board's first year of tram replacement came to an end, it had commenced five new routes, converted two depots over to trolleybus operation, finished the task at Fulwell and built a new depot. It had taken into stock 113 new vehicles and the standard had been set. The task ahead was a formidable one.

Left:
'B1' No 64 is on trial at Crystal Palace prior to the opening of route 654. The new roundabout is under construction.
Omnibus Society

January arrived, and former LUT No 61 visited Brighton for demonstration purposes at the time when the town was considering the options for tram replacement. Back in London, however, there was a new sign of the times. The tram map for 1936 was renamed 'Trolleybus and Tram map' and new editions appeared regularly throughout the year, showing all the new routes. Further new Bills were submitted to Parliament, requesting powers to operate routes covering Waltham Cross and Enfield, as well as Barnet, Hampstead, Moorgate, Smithfield, Holborn and sections from West Croydon to Scrubs Lane, and a loop at Wandsworth. The final 'B1s' were delivered in January, enabling Sutton to extend its route to Crystal Palace.

Things were quiet in February, although work was proceeding at Stonebridge Park for the next stage of the changeover, but, as it was to prove, not quickly enough. The next few vehicles to arrive did so in March, in the shape of the first seven of the class 'C2' and three 'C3s'. All were based on the AEC 664T chassis and had English Electric motors and control equipment, but the bodywork was supplied by Metro-Cammell in the case of the 'C2s', and by BRCW in the case of the 'C3s'. All were built with half-width bulkheads and were 70-seaters. The Metro-Cammell and the BRCW bodies

CHAPTER 2
1936

Below:
Acton depot had a short affair with the trolleybus, when Stonebridge Park was not ready in time. A former London United tram, numbered 2357 by the Board, appears to be ready for the 55, while new trolleybus No 277 visits, no doubt to show the staff what the future holds.

were very similar in appearance. The 'C2s' were numbered 184-283, and the 'C3s' 284-383. The 'C2s' and 'C3s' had 99 of their number fitted with rear wheel covers, known as spats, and were especially attractive.

Seventeen 'C2s' and five 'C3s' were delivered in April and on the 5th of that month the conversions were under way again. Stonebridge was not ready in time, and so Acton depot played host to the new trolleybuses when they commenced new route 660 between Acton and Hammersmith over the former LUT lines.

Another arrival in April from Lancashire was the first all-Leyland-built London trolleybus, 'D1' class No 384 — the chassis was designated LPTB70. It was basically similar to the 'C' class vehicles in appearance, but the electrical equipment was by Metrovick. The vehicle was also fitted with rear wheel spats, the only Leyland to be so treated, and had a half-width bulkhead and provision for 70 seats. Initially sent to Bexley, it figured heavily

in Leyland's publicity of the day, being photographed extensively at several locations on route 696 and appearing in its trolleybus sales brochure issued that year.

Twenty-four 'C2s' and a further 11 'C3s' came in May, and work was nearing completion at Hendon, Stonebridge and Finchley for the next round of changes. The former MET depot at Stonebridge was to provide the drivers' training school and, as already mentioned, had a circuit wired around the depot for this purpose. Hendon received new office accommodation, an extension to the main shed for the new trolleybuses and turning space at the rear. This former MET shed had been the scene of possibly the first trolleybus trial in Britain, when a single-decker was tried in 1909. The other depot to feature, also once MET, was Finchley, which had been extended over former permanent way land and also had a traverser added.

Only one 'C2' arrived in June, but a flood of new trolleybuses came in July — 25 'C2s' and

28 'C3s' — and on 5 July the attack on the former MET routes commenced. On this date, new route 666 from Edgware to Hammersmith commenced, operated by Acton, Hendon and Stonebridge Park, and the 660 service was suspended until 2 August, when it was reintroduced to run from North Finchley to Hammersmith (served by Finchley and Stonebridge depots). On the same day new route 645 began running from North Finchley to Edgware (served by Finchley and Colindale depots), and again for all these changes the new 'C2s' were used, 25 'C2s' and 29 'C3s' having been received during August. On the 23rd of the same month, yet more old MET tram routes came to the end of the line, when new routes 662 from Paddington Green to Sudbury, and 664 between Paddington Green and Edgware started. The 662 was operated by Stonebridge and the 664 by Stonebridge and Hendon. This meant the end of trams at Hendon and Stonebridge, and during the summer Hendon works yard became available as a scrapyard. Away from the transport scene in July, the Government had taken steps to prepare for mass production of gas masks, a frightening warning of what was already believed to be an uncertain future.

While these events were taking place, the Bill submitted to Parliament earlier in the year was passed, paving the way for more activity. In September, a further 10 of the earlier short-wheelbase vehicles were received. These all had BRCW bodies and Metrovick equipment; Nos 489-493 were identical to the batch numbered 64-93 and classified 'B1', but Nos 484-488, classified 'B3', differed in that they did not have special brakes. These were intended as spares for the earlier batches, but in fact they were used initially as training vehicles. A further four 'C3s' were also delivered this month.

October saw the introduction of yet another class, the 'D2s'. Like the lone 'D1', they were Leyland LPTB70s with Metrovick electrics, but the bodies came from Metro-Cammell and did not have the handsome rear wheel spats that were so popular. These vehicles were very much like the 'C2s', although they had an opening front nearside window and deeper rainshields above the windows. Ten were delivered that month and the class were numbered 385-483. Like the 'D1', they had half-width bulkheads and 70 seats. Deliveries of the 'C2s' and 'C3s' were nearly complete when another 10 'C3s' came in October, the last of

Opposite:
'C2' No 223 was delivered in May 1936 and is seen here with others at Hendon. The former MET trams on the left had only a few months to go.
D. W. K. Jones

Left:
'C3' No 314 has just worked short to Golders Green from North Finchley, and awaits the return trip in the summer rain. It is August 1936 and route 645 has just come into existence.
Omnibus Society

Above:
The second batch of short-wheelbase trolleybuses arrived in September 1936. They consisted of two groups of five vehicles classed 'B3' and 'B1', and were Leylands with BRCW bodywork. No 492 is seen here in postwar years at Moorgate. *Alan Cross*

Right:
Route 662 started in August and 'C1' No 158 seems to have strayed from its usual haunts at Fulwell and Hounslow to operate from Stonebridge Park. This view is at Paddington Green.

Opposite above:
The next Leylands to arrive were the 'D2s'. These carried MCCW bodies and began the new 607 when it started in November 1936. No 433, seen here, was delivered in that month, although this picture shows the vehicle basking in the sun of spring 1937 at Shepherds Bush.

Opposite below:
Overhead is erected in Church Road, Leyton, in readiness for future conversions. The crews are assisted by one of the new tower wagons and by one of the converted NS type buses.
C. Carter

these classes not being received into stock until the new year.

The next area for the Board's attention was to the northeast of London, when the former Walthamstow Corporation depot was the centre of attention on 18 October and trolleybuses were to operate over roads previously unserved by trams. Route 623 worked from Woodford to Manor House, and used the proposed Tottenham to Walthamstow tram route which had finally been approved by the Ministry of Transport in 1930 but never built. The long-awaited link between the Metropolitan Electric and Walthamstow Corporation was at last a reality; again 'C3' vehicles were used.

The arrival of 62 new 'D2s' in November allowed the conversion at Hanwell to go ahead. The building work here was not yet complete; new offices, a traverser and a new doorway to allow through working via Jessamine Road were still in progress, and so Acton depot was also used on 15 November, when 'D2s' began work on a new route 607 from Uxbridge to Shepherds Bush. When a further seven 'D2s' arrived in December, Hanwell had enough to begin work on route 655 from Craven Park to Hammersmith on the 13th. This conversion meant the end of the old LUT network, apart from the short stretch from Wimbledon to Tooting.

To go back to the subject of Leyland publicity, the *Leyland Journal* of December 1936 states 'London Transport have risen to the proud position of being the largest operator in the World of Trolleybuses. At the time of writing, their drivers and conductors total 1,600 and this figure is constantly rising.' The journal goes on to question the effect of the trolleybus on traffic congestion, and the spokesman for LT is reported as saying, 'We would operate trolleys anywhere. The trolleybus is essentially a flexible vehicle.' It is interesting to note the change in the context of the word 'flexible' when statements were made in the 1950s on the abandonment announcement.

And so 1936 drew to its close. Eight new routes had commenced, four depots had lost their trams, and two — Finchley and Walthamstow — had received their first trolleybuses. In all, 286 new vehicles had been taken into stock and more of the same was to follow.

Right:
London Road at Crayford, and the only 'D1', No 384, makes its way to Woolwich on route 696. This was the first Leyland 30-footer and Leyland made much of it in its publicity of the day. This and several other views were taken for the 1936 brochure on 6 June.
©The British Commercial Vehicle Museum Trust Archives

The country was just coming to terms with the abdication of King Edward VIII in December 1936, when the last 10 'C3s' and the final 'C2' were delivered during January with eight more 'D2s'. These vehicles were enough to enable Walthamstow to commence new route 685, between Crooked Billet and Markhouse Road, on 17 January, and take a second swipe at the former Corporation routes.

February was a quiet month, with only half a dozen new 'D2s' taken into stock, but March was to prove more interesting. Two more 'D2s' came and the first of the new 'E' classes was received, in the shape of 'E3' No 629, and the first 'F1', No 654. The 'E3' class were based on the AEC 664T chassis, with English Electric motors and Metrovick controllers, and carried the first bodies to be built by Park Royal for the trolleybus fleet. The most obvious distinguishing feature of these bodies was the double row of four ventilators

set above the windscreen, the only class to have them. They were numbered 629-653.

The 'F1s' were an all-Leyland product and were the first from that factory to have 70-seater bodies with full-width bulkheads, apart from Nos 654-664, which were half-width. These bodies were similar to that of No 384, although deeper rainshields were fitted and the doorway was slightly lower than previous classes. No 674 differed in that it had side

CHAPTER 3
1937

Below:
A sight for sore eyes. Leyland's inspection shop on 30 July 1937 sees six new 'F1s', Nos 694-699, lined up ready for delivery after final checks. The 'F1s' were an all-Leyland product and were to grace Uxbridge Road for over 20 years.
©*The British Commercial Vehicle Museum Trust Archives*

lights set into the front dash, rather than mounted on the sides as on the rest of the class. Their motors and control equipment were by Metrovick, and they were numbered from 654 to 753. As they trickled into stock, they were sent to Hanwell depot, where they gradually replaced 'D2s'.

On 9 March Acton depot closed its doors to trolleybuses for the last time, as rebuilding work was completed elsewhere — route 666 had been transferred from the depot on 13 December 1936. It had been an operational depot for less than a year.

April saw one more 'D2' and the first four arrivals of the 'E2' class, along with three more 'F1s'. The 'E2' specification was the same as the 'E3s', but the bodywork came from Weymann's of Addlestone. Like the 'E3s' and all standard trolleybuses thereafter, it featured full-width bulkheads and provision for 70 seats. The 'E2s' carried the fleet numbers 604-628 and their most significant difference from the other bodies was the split rear dome, most others having a single, one-piece construction.

The Board's enthusiastic approach to experimentation also emerged in April, when class 'X4' No 754 was unveiled to the public. It was the first stab at a chassisless trolleybus and used AEC running units fitted to a light underframe, to which the body side girders were fixed. Metrovick supplied the motor and control equipment, but the body was built by LPTB itself at Charlton works. This body was unique because as well as the usual rear open platform, it had a front exit with folding doors. Although this reduced the seating by four, two seats were regained by fitting a half-width bulkhead and positioning a seat for two, facing the driver. The cream band between decks was a metal strip fixed to the body; the only vehicle so treated, it lacked the usual black lining out on this band. The vehicle was delivered to

Finchley, where it spent its entire working life. The front exit was not used in later years.

On 12 May, away from the transport scene, the nation prepared to settle down by their wireless sets and listen to the coronation of King George VI.

May also saw a bus strike. This meant greatly increased revenue for the Tram & Trolleybus Department, as they were not involved in the dispute. The last three 'D2s' came, and the first 'D3' arrived in this month, when No 494 was delivered. The class was numbered 494-553 and, like the 'D1' and 'D2' classes, was based on Leyland chassis with Metrovick motors and control equipment but with bodywork by BRCW. The main difference between the 'D2s' and 'D3s' was that the latter were built with full-width bulkheads from new.

The same month saw another new class emerge in the shape of the 'E1s'. Like the previous 'E' class vehicles, they had AEC 664T chassis with English Electric motors and Metrovick controllers, but were fitted with bodywork by Brush, which was similar to the 'E3s', although the front corner pillars

Below:
No 606 was one of four 'E2s' delivered in April 1937. These were Weymann-bodied AECs which spent their lives at work in the East End.

Bottom:
In April another experimental vehicle took to the road in the shape of 'X4' No 754. This had a traditional open platform entrance, but a front exit, provided with folding doors. The body was built at Charlton works, and the Board combined with AEC to provide the fleet with this chassisless vehicle. It spent all of its life at Finchley depot, and is seen here operating in Finchley on the 621 in postwar days. *C. Carter*

were not as thick as the Park Royal products. Again, all were fitted with full-width bulkheads, with the exception of No 554, which was half-width. The class was numbered 554-603, and 12 were delivered in May, along with 20 'E2s', 23 'E3s' and eight 'F1s'.

The only other significant event during the month was the introduction of new route 694 between Erith and Woolwich via Welling, but this did not involve any new wiring. It commenced on the 16th. It is interesting to note that about this time London Transport rented space in the old East Ham tram depot in Nelson Street, to store new trolleybus overhead equipment during the East London conversions. It had inherited the depot in July 1933 but had then sold it back to the Corporation in December 1935, surplus to requirements.

June arrived and with it came seven 'E1s', one 'E2', one 'E3', one 'F1' and nine 'D3s', and there were now enough new vehicles to start the next assault on the East End. On 6 June Walthamstow finally lost its last tram, and West Ham became involved for the first time, when four new routes began. They were the 669 from Stratford Broadway to Canning Town and three routes from Chingford Mount to Victoria & Albert Docks — the 687 via Leyton and

Wanstead, the 697 via Leyton and Abbey Arms and the 699 via Leyton and Greengate. All were jointly operated apart from the 669, which was the sole responsibility of West Ham. The operation of specials between West Ham Stadium and Plaistow was, however, retained as a tram route until July 1938. This latest conversion utilised some 'D2s' along with some of the 'B3s' delivered in September 1936, as well as 'E' class vehicles.

Summer came, and as the nation was introduced to the new 999 telephone emergency service on 1 July, the month also brought one 'D3' and two 'F1s'. August was more productive, however: 25 gleaming new 'D3s' from Birmingham, 49 'F1s' from Leyland and 13 more 'E1s' from the Brush factory at Loughborough. A point to mention here is the delay in delivery of 'F1' No 661 from Leyland. This vehicle sustained severe damage to the roof in an incident at the factory and was not ready for delivery until June.

After the summer holidays the conversion was under way again on 12 September, when an east/west attack was mounted, with West Ham, Hammersmith and Wandsworth the targets. At West Ham route 689 began

operating a circular route from Stratford Broadway to East Ham via a loop which was worked in both directions. This was also operated by 'E' class vehicles, most of which were destined to stay at West Ham for all their working lives.

The western part of the conversion brought in new routes: 626 between Clapham Junction and Acton, 628 from Clapham Junction to Craven Park, and 630 from Scrubs Lane to West Croydon, all operated by Hammersmith, and the 612 from Battersea to Mitcham, operated by Wandsworth. Hammersmith depot

Opposite above:
Very rarely did the former London United Diddlers venture onto the 667, but it happened in May 1937, thanks to the Coronation. No 9 is waiting on the stand at Hammersmith. *R. Newell*

Opposite below:
The first of the 'E1s' came in May, and here at the Brush factory in Loughborough is No 570, destined to start work in the East End and face some of the fiercest air raids of the war. *Brush of Loughborough, courtesy Leicestershire Records Office*

Above:
This is the junction at Markhouse Road in May 1937; as can be seen, the work is almost complete for the new routes. *London Transport*

was being extensively rebuilt at this time and during this early period some vehicles for routes 626 and 628 were outstationed at Chiswick tram depot. The 'D2s' that had moved out of Hanwell and Acton were drafted into Hammersmith to work these routes, along with some newer 'D3s', which also went to Wandsworth for the 612. Four roads were made available inside Wandsworth depot for trolleybuses, an allocation which was not increased, as the depot was destined never to extend its trolleybus operations. This West London conversion was unique in that it was the first time the former LCC conduit routes were affected, all previous conversions featuring overhead supply routes. On 12 September the 685 was extended from Markhouse Road south to Canning Town.

During September four more 'E1s', five 'D3s' and nine 'F1s' were taken into stock. October brought a further seven 'F1s' and in November 14 'E1s', 19 'D3s' and 15 'F1s' arrived. On 14 December, to help bewildered passengers in the East Ham area, vehicles operating on the anticlockwise loop of route 689 started to show route number 690.

As 1937 drew to a close, the final five 'F1s' came into stock. Walthamstow and Hammersmith had lost their last trams, and West Ham and Wandsworth had seen their first trolleybuses, 12 new routes had commenced, 292 new vehicles had been delivered, route mileage had reached 147, and the Board was poised for an even more hectic 1938.

Top right:
'E2' No 609 was delivered in May, and on 6 June route 669 was born. The scene here is North Woolwich, previously unserved by trams, and only reached by the trolleybus in February 1938. *Omnibus Society*

Centre right:
The photographer seems to have sneaked up on 'F1' No 678 as it rests on the Uxbridge stand ready for the long run back to Shepherds Bush. It shares the stand with a Green Line T. The date is around October 1937. *Omnibus Society*

Right:
Route 612 commenced in September 1937, and 'D3' No 509 seen here was delivered a month earlier. It glides through the dismal rain, while a horse and carriage can be seen in the distance. *Omnibus Society*

The year started quietly, with no new vehicles arriving in January. Frank Pick inspected overhead equipment, which included some made by the Ohio Brass Co. As a result of this, some of the fittings were used in Wood Green High Road, the Wood Green turning loop and in the depot itself. Most of this lasted until just after the war, and the last was replaced by 1953.

Parliament was approached for yet more powers, this time to operate routes along Highgate High Street, North Hill and Southwood Lane to East Finchley.

Things got moving again in February. New trolleybuses arrived *en masse* and yet more new classes were introduced to London: 54 'H1s', 32 'J1s', eight 'J2s' and the prototype 'M1' No 953 were delivered. The 'H1s', numbered 755-904, were Leylands with Metro-Cammell bodywork and Metrovick electrical equipment. This class set a new precedent for the rest of the fleet, in that the power cables were now fed through the first upper deck side pillar and not through two pillars as on earlier vehicles, resulting in a wider first pillar. Another change was the front grilles receiving louvres rather than mesh as previously fitted. Apart from this, the 'H1s' were very similar to the 'D2s'.

CHAPTER 4
1938

Below:
'B1' No 90 tries out the new wiring at the junction of Woodhouse Road and Great North Road, North Finchley, in February 1938, prior to the new services which began a month later. A member of the crew of tower wagon No 200, later to be renumbered 88Q, is in attendance. *D. W. K. Jones*

The 'J1s' were numbered 905-952 and were AEC 664T chassis with Weymann bodies, apart from No 952 which came from Metro-Cammell. All of the 'J' classes had Metrovick motors with English Electric controllers. The 'J2s' were Nos 955-1029, and again were AEC 664Ts, but this time with BRCW bodywork.

The prototype 'M1' was an experiment by AEC in unit construction, based on its 664T chassis. Weymann built the body, which was the first to incorporate radiused front upper deck windows and the only one to employ a single-piece front destination screen. The electrical equipment was supplied by Metrovick. The vehicle was delivered to West Ham, where it remained for all of its short life.

Back to the conversion front, and on 6 February Ilford depot lost its trams in favour of 'E1' trolleybuses, which began new routes 691 from Barking to Barkingside and 693 from Barking to Chadwell Heath. On the same date, the 669 was extended south to North Woolwich, along roads previously unserved by trams. On 12 February route 692 began operating between Chadwell Heath and The

Above opposite:
Prototype 'M1' No 953 does not appear to have been photographed very often in its very short life. The unit-constructed AEC with Weymann body had a unique front blind layout, and is seen here at Fulwell depot in February 1938 after delivery. It was allocated to West Ham, where it stayed until it was burnt out in fog in 1943 and subsequently scrapped.

Below opposite:
'E1' No 588 turns right at the Old Chequers, Barkingside, on route 691, which started in February 1938. The vehicle was delivered in the previous September, and this view dates from about May 1938. *Omnibus Society*

Above:
Route 692 commenced on 12 February 1938 and had disappeared by 3 December the same year. 'E1' No 587 is seen here at Newbury Park in about May, the bus having been taken into stock in September 1937. *Omnibus Society*

Horns, on Saturday afternoons and evenings, also operated by Ilford.

March came, and with it another 25 'H1s', three 'J1s' and four 'J2s', along with the prototype 'L2', No 954. This bus was similar to the 'H1s' in appearance, with bodywork by Metro-Cammell and Metrovick electrical equipment, but the vehicle was an AEC chassisless design, very similar to No 754. Its most distinguishing feature was the lower deck cream band, which extended around the front of the vehicle, below the driver's cab.

In the wider world, there were more signs of what was to come in the years ahead, when in March the Government announced that it was to spend £11 million on new airfields for the RAF.

6 March was the date in the conversion calendar when Finchley lost its last trams and Holloway was introduced to the trolleybus for the first time. Finchley received 'J1s' and 'J2s', while Holloway had some 'H1s'. These together began new routes 609 from Barnet to Moorgate and 617 from North Finchley to Holborn via Highgate, operated by Holloway, and 521/621 from North Finchley to Holborn via Finsbury Park and 651 from Barnet to Cricklewood, operated by Finchley. They were

the first routes to use the 500 series numbers, and in this instance they denoted the direction travelled round the loop at Holborn, the 600 series operating in a clockwise direction, and the 500 series anticlockwise.

The following day, 7 March, route 517 began to follow its fellow 617, but in the opposite direction round the loop. With this stage, the trams' last great hope in the shape of the 'Felthams' were transferred south to Telford Avenue to see out their London lives, before leaving for another life in Leeds. During the preparation for this conversion there were protests at the siting of traction poles outside Staple Inn in Holborn, a listed building, and eventually the Board relented and repositioned them. The trolleybus had at last entered central London.

During March a programme to rebuild the half-width bulkhead vehicles into full-width began at Charlton and Fulwell. All of the 'B', 'C', 'D' and the few 'E' and 'F' classes were dealt with, and they were completed by the end of the year, with the exception of No 445 which had already had its body strengthened and retained its half-width bulkhead to the end.

The two seats removed from the position opposite the driver in this conversion were relocated on the upper deck rear offside, to maintain the overall seating capacity. The exceptions to this were Nos 385-444 and 446-482, which received only a single seat upstairs, reducing their capacity to 69.

Another healthy intake of vehicles came in April, when 33 'H1s', 13 'J1s' and 28 'J2s' were delivered in readiness for the next changes, which were to take place on 8 May and brought Wood Green into the trolleybus network. It shared the operation of new route 625 from Wood Green to Walthamstow with Walthamstow depot, and operated exclusively the 629 from Enfield to Tottenham Court Road and the 641 from Winchmore Hill to Moorgate.

Below:
The date is 17 June 1938 and 'J1' No 916 had appeared in February 1938, ready to begin the new routes in March. It is seen here at North Finchley on the 617. 'H1' No 801, behind on the 609, later had its body destroyed at Bexleyheath in 1944. It was subsequently rebodied by East Lancs.

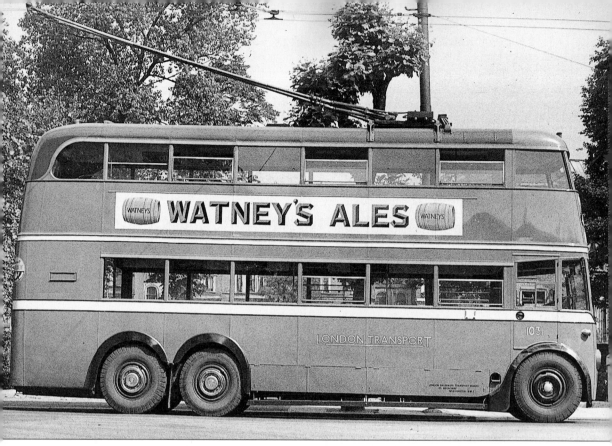

The Board had difficulty in establishing a turning point at Tottenham Court Road. It favoured Bedford Square but too many wealthy occupants objected, so eventually it had to settle for a turn at Howland Street, travelling in a square via Fitzroy Street and Maple Street, falling short of the area that the Board had wished to reach. Now for the first time trolleybus mileage exceeded that of the trams, and this conversion meant that the routes in the east and west of London were now linked and it was possible to travel from North Woolwich and Woodford in the east to Uxbridge and Hounslow in the west, without using a motorbus.

Behind the scenes during May another order was placed, for a further 315 trolleybuses, 175 of which were to be chassisless and all of which were to be manufactured by AEC. Also in May, an incident of interest took place at Shepherds Bush, where, due to road subsidence, southbound 626, 628 and 630s were diverted around the Green, before resuming their normal route down Shepherds Bush Road. This was before the Green had adopted the one-way system, which came into operation at the end of the year. May deliveries were 11 'H1s' and five 'J2s'.

On 1 June the 645 was extended at both ends, to Canons Park and Barnet, and as a result route 651 was withdrawn, thus becoming the shortest-lived London trolleybus

Opposite above:
The 'J3' class were also AECs with BRCW bodies but were fitted with coasting and runback brakes for the operation of route 611 on Highgate Hill. No 1031 is seen here in July 1946, posing for a publicity picture. *London Transport*

Opposite below:
'J2' No 1011 was delivered in June 1938 and was an AEC with bodywork by BRCW. This view, dated 13 July 1939 at King's Cross, shows the drivers wearing their summer whites.

Below:
The body erecting shop at the Leyland factory on 31 October 1938, and nine 'K' class vehicles can be seen nearing completion.
©*The British Commercial Vehicle Museum Trust Archives*

route. The month's deliveries consisted of 30 'J2s' and 21 'H1s'. Holloway was the only participant on 10 July, when 'H1s', 'J2s' and 'B3s' (the latter coming from West Ham) began routes 513/613, Hampstead Heath to Parliament Hill Fields via the Holborn loop, 615 Parliament Hill Fields to Moorgate, and 639 from Hampstead Heath to Moorgate. Also on that date Hampstead tram depot ceased to operate as a running shed.

The summer of 1938 was a quiet one for the trolleybus, with only five 'J3s' and four 'H1s' coming into ownership. The 'J3s' were again AEC 664Ts with BRCW bodies, Metrovick motors and English Electric controllers, but differed from the 'J2s' in that they were fitted with coasting and runback brakes, which were deemed necessary for Highgate Hill. Of the 25 to be built, numbered 1030-1054, No 1054 stood out from the rest, having a modified front end. It was more sloped than the remainder of the class and had a similar look to the 'N1' class, which followed just over a year later.

September arrived and everybody celebrated when Prime Minister Neville Chamberlain came back from his Munich meeting with Hitler to announce there would be 'peace in our time'. In October the conversions were under way again. On the 16th, Holloway and Edmonton were at the centre of operations, when new routes 659 from Waltham Cross to Holborn Circus, 679 from Smithfield to Ponders End (Waltham Cross on Sundays) and 649 from Ponders End to Stamford Hill, began; Edmonton operated on all routes and Holloway helped on the 679.

The final two 'H1s', 20 more 'J3s' and 19 'Ks' came into stock in October, the 'J3s' going to Holloway and the others to Edmonton for the new routes. The 'K' class vehicles were an all-Leyland product, fitted with Metrovick motors, the controllers being Metrovick in the case of the 'K1s' and English Electric in the 'K2s'. The 'K1s' were numbered 1055-1154 and 1255-1304, and the 'K2s' were 1155-1254 and 1305-1354. They were similar in appearance to the 'F1s' and were extremely durable vehicles, and also the largest class of trolleybus to be purchased by the Board.

November was a sad month for the tram enthusiast, when the final former MET routes disappeared. Fifty 'K' class trolleybuses arrived from Lancashire, and on 6 November route 627 from Tottenham Court Road to Edmonton began, operated by Holloway. 'K' class Leylands were used for this change, along with the last few 'H1s'. On 3 December route 692 was withdrawn, after serving the public for less than a year, with the 691 and 693 augmented in its place. The final deliveries in that month were 27 more 'K' class Leylands.

To sum up the year, 20 new routes had commenced, although one was prematurely withdrawn, 396 new vehicles had been taken into stock, by far the biggest intake in any one year, and four more depots had joined the list. The trams were being swept aside.

Top:
October 1938, and 'K1' No 1062 is about to be delivered to Edmonton depot by breakdown tender No AN31. The driver is no doubt checking that the coast is clear before turning right into Tramway Avenue. *D. W. K. Jones*

Above:
Posed, but still very nice, is 'K1' No 1127 at Leyland on 28 December 1938. Although obviously complete, the vehicle wasn't officially delivered until the following February.
©*The British Commercial Vehicle Museum Trust Archives*

The new year started quietly on the vehicle front, as only five more 'K' types were delivered in January, but February saw an acceleration in deliveries, with 73 more of the Leylands arriving. The new routes featured on the 5th of that month were the 647 from Stamford Hill to London Docks and the 649 extension to Liverpool Street. On the 6th, the 643 from Wood Green to the Holborn loop and the 683 from Stamford Hill to Moorgate commenced. Stamford Hill depot featured exclusively in this conversion and 'K' class Leylands were used on the new routes.

On 5 March the heavily used tram route 53 was replaced by the 653 between Tottenham Court Road and Aldgate, worked to begin with by the 'K' types from Holloway, although they were replaced by the 'L' classes which arrived in later months. These vehicles used the newly opened Aldgate bus station at Minories.

Vehicle deliveries for March were 53 'Ks' and two of the new class 'L1'. The 'L1s' were MCW chassisless vehicles with AEC units and Metrovick motors. Their controllers were by English Electric and bodywork was by Metro-Cammell, and they were numbered 1355-1369. These buses were fitted with coasting and runback brakes for future use on Highgate Hill. Four 'L1s' were delivered in April and, on the 7th, route 543 began between Wood Green

CHAPTER 5
1939 AND THE WAR YEARS

Below:
The body mounting shop at Leyland's factory on 5 April 1939, and several lower decks, together with an upper, can be seen in various states of painting. They were all to form part of the 300 'K1' and 'K2' class vehicles, which were delivered between October 1938 and June 1939.
©The British Commercial Vehicle Museum Trust Archives

and the Holborn loop, travelling in the reverse direction round the loop to the 643. From this date the 643 went one way round the loop, the 543 the other. Before then, the 643 went both ways.

Three 'L1s' and a solitary 'K' came in May, but June saw the next changes. On the 11th, routes 555 from Bloomsbury to Leyton Green, 557 between Liverpool Street and Chingford Mount, and 581 from Bloomsbury to Woodford were introduced. Leyton and Hackney shared the 555 and 581; Walthamstow operated the 557 and some 581s. 'K' class Leylands again were used throughout this conversion.

Fulwell's yard was a very busy place in June, when 72 'Ks', six 'L1s', nine 'L2s', three 'N1s' and the experimental 'X5' were all delivered. The 'L2s' were numbered 1370-1378 and had the same specification as the 'L1s', except that they did not have runback brakes. The 'N1s' were AEC 664Ts with BRCW bodies, Metrovick motors and English Electric controllers. They were numbered 1555-1644.

Without doubt the most interesting new vehicle was 'X5' No 1379. Again the specification was as the 'L2s' but this vehicle was intended as a prototype for a class of trolleybuses to operate through the Kingsway subway.

The stations in the subway had centre island loading platforms and therefore the vehicle needed an offside loading facility as well as the usual nearside one. No 1379 was fitted with a rear offside jack-knife door, and a straight staircase, to allow boarding at Holborn and Aldwych stations. The overall appearance was very similar to the other 'L' class buses, except that the rear was very flat and rather ugly in comparison. Seating was for 68. Runback brakes were fitted, due to the steep incline of the northern ramp of the subway, and provision for a 'via Kingsway Subway' board was made on the front dome.

It made only two round trips through the subway, on 13 August, with the lower seating removed to accommodate extra batteries and air cylinders. The batteries were insufficient for the first trip and power was exhausted before the return journey could be completed. It was therefore towed back to the Bloomsbury end by lorry. After a run under the wires in North London to recharge the batteries, it returned for a second trip but with exactly the same outcome and the scheme appears to have died fairly soon afterwards. Clearances were very tight in the subway and alterations throughout would no doubt have

been very costly. The vehicle did enter service, and spent its entire working life at Holloway.

As the summer came, there were more ominous rumblings across Europe, and the country was coming to terms with what looked to be inevitable. Chamberlain confirmed Britain's pledge to stand by Poland.

Opposite above:
The 'L2' class was also an AEC/MCCW chassisless batch of vehicles, only nine in number. No 1377 is seen here at Moorgate, Finsbury Square, on route 615. It was delivered in June 1939.

Opposite below:
No 1366 was one of the 15 'L1' AEC/MCCW chassisless vehicles, all fitted with coasting and runback brakes for Highgate Hill. This is June 1939, and the vehicle has just been delivered. It stands at King's Cross on route 615, and the drivers are now wearing their summer uniforms.

Above:
'X5' No 1379 was the experimental Kingsway subway trolleybus with the offside platform doors. Although it made two trips through the subway, this was never persevered with and it was destined to remain at Holloway depot for its operational life until withdrawn in March 1955.

News on the vehicle front was very slow, with only seven new 'N1s' arriving in July and just one of the new 'L3s' taken into stock in August. The 'L3s' were the largest class of chassisless trolleybuses to be built for London. They were MCW with AEC running units, Metrovick motors and controllers and Metro-Cammell bodywork, numbered 1380-1529. Two of the class, Nos 1500 and 1515, were originally fitted with automatic acceleration.

The expected happened on 3 September, when Britain declared war on Germany, and the nation prepared itself for the predicted bomb and gas attacks. Only seven days later, on the 10th, route 677 commenced between West India Dock and Smithfield, operated by 'K' types from Hackney.

A very interesting acquisition was made in September. This was class 'X7' No 1671, which had been a Leyland demonstrator and consequently had a Lancashire registration. The number therefore did not correspond with the fleet number, as was London practice. The vehicle, built in February, was an all-Leyland chassisless product with Metrovick motor and controller, but the big difference from the rest of the fleet was that it was a twin-steering bus with a single rear axle. The internal difference was that the longitudinal seats in the lower saloon were at the front of the vehicle. It spent its early life at Fulwell before moving to Hanwell.

Other deliveries in September were 20 'L3s' and 19 'N1s'. October brought in another six 'L3s', but in November 18 more arrived, together with four 'M1s', 40 'N1s' and 22 'N2s'. At the outbreak of war, London's tram fleet had shrunk to just over 1,100.

The 'M1s' were AEC/MCW unit constructed, to an AEC design using a light steel chassis frame with crossmembers coinciding with outriggers, connected to the body pillars, giving greater rigidity and lighter construction. The motors were Metrovick,

Opposite above:
New in June 1940, No 1526 was one of the chassisless 'L3' vehicles with MCCW bodies. Although the first batch went to Holloway, the class will always be associated with the East End routes of Poplar and West Ham in their early years. This view is at Barking. *Omnibus Society*

Opposite below:
No 1671 was perhaps the most unusual trolleybus in the fleet. It started life as a Leyland demonstrator in February 1939, and consequently was registered in Lancashire. When it was acquired that September, it became the only vehicle in the fleet, apart from the former LUT vehicles and prototypes, whose registration number did not correspond with its fleet number. The twin-steering layout was to remain unique in the fleet, and the bus was withdrawn in May 1955. *Alan Cross*

Above:
The 661 was a 5 November route, and the new 'N2' class shared the Bow workings with its AEC 'N1' brothers. No 1659 was received in November and stands here at Aldgate, prior to the run back to Leyton depot. *Omnibus Society*

Top:
Bonfire Night 1939 saw the start of route 663 and the Bow operations. 'N1' No 1610, delivered the same month, can be seen here at Aldgate sporting the wartime white markings, although the headlamp masking does not appear to be complete yet. The anti-blast window mesh was to come later. *Omnibus Society*

controllers were English Electric and the bodywork was by Weymann. They were numbered 1530-1554. The 'N2s' were 'back to basics' AEC 664T chassis with Metrovick motors, English Electric controllers and Park Royal bodies, with a very distinctive front dome and thick corner pillars. They were very different from the earlier 'E3' class, which Park Royal had supplied. The rear dome was of split construction, as the previous 'E2s', and the doorway was lower than that of the 'N1s'. They carried the numbers 1645-1669.

The 'N' class trolleybuses were used on Bonfire Night to start Bow's new routes 661 from Aldgate to Leyton and 663 from Aldgate to Ilford. There was a strike at Hanwell over the running times being too short, as the crews now claimed that they had extra passengers to carry due to the reductions in bus services made in September.

In December, 15 'M1s' came with 16 'L3s', and on the 10th Holloway was cleared of its tram route 11, when route 611 began running from Highgate Village to Moorgate. The delay of over a year since the last Holloway conversion was due to objections by residents to wiring in the select Highgate village, only

resolved when LT bought land for use as a turning point and stand. The terminal was just short of that served by the trams. Tickets for the new route had been printed for some time and several were used on the last days of the trams, due to a shortage of route 11 tickets. 'J3s' and 'L1s' were used and the regulations stated that the coasting brake must be engaged at the compulsory stop after leaving the terminus, and that no standing passengers were allowed on the descent of Highgate Hill. Highgate was to retain the rest of its trams until April 1952, thus operating the two forms of electric transport for 14 years.

By the end of the year, 401 new vehicles had been received.

1940 dawned, and the public were immediately faced with rationing of butter, bacon and sugar. LT took into stock two 'L3's, six 'M1s', two 'N2s' and the experimental class 'X6' No 1670. This vehicle was English Electric's contribution to the chassisless classes. It built the 68-seat bodywork and joined with AEC in supplying the frame, running units and control equipment, while a Metrovick motor was used. Due to the method of its construction, the bulkhead was set further back, resulting in the loss of two seats in the lower saloon. It was allocated to West Ham.

At this time, Charlton works engineering shops were given over to the Ministry of Defence for the manufacture of munitions and gun parts, and played a very significant part in the war effort.

February came and 10 more 'N1s' arrived, followed in March by four 'L3s' and five 'N1s', but April and May were very quiet months for the trolleybus fleet. More significant happenings at the time were the invasion of Belgium, Luxembourg and the Netherlands by Germany in May, and the resignation of Chamberlain with the subsequent formation of the National Government under the leadership of Winston Churchill. The month culminated in the rescue of over 330,000 men from the beaches of Dunkirk.

With this as the backdrop, what turned out to be the last tram to trolleybus conversion took place on 9 June. Poplar depot had been enlarged by using former permanent way land to the rear of the depot, and was ready to begin route 565 from the Holborn loop to East

Ham, the 567 from Aldgate to West Ham, and the 665 from Bloomsbury to Barking. The operations were shared with West Ham. The 567 was extended to Barking on Saturday evenings and worked from Poplar to Smithfield on Sundays. 'L3s' and some 'M1s' were used for this occasion.

June also saw the delivery of 83 more 'L3s', six 'N1s' and a solitary 'N2', by which time 1,671 trolleybuses were in stock. At this point, deliveries were halted for some months.

The first disruption to the system during the war came on 16 August, when wires were brought down in an air raid at Malden. Repairs were said to have been completed in four hours.

The 7 September marked the beginning of the bombing campaign on the docks and they were mercilessly pounded for 76 consecutive nights, apart from 2 November, when bad weather intervened. On 7 September No 1565 from Bow had its body damaged beyond repair, as did No 1128 from Stamford Hill on the 18th and No 107 from Holloway on the 27th. They would all be rebodied later. No 1246 was also damaged at Hackney but survived after having its roof rebuilt to a flatter style than the rest of the fleet.

Anti-blast netting was now being applied but it was to take nearly a year to complete the fleet. Vehicles also had white paint applied to the front mudguards and rear bumpers to assist in the blackout, and motorbuses were painted with a white circle on the rear lower panel, so that trolleybus drivers could tell at once which vehicles they could safely overtake.

In October new deliveries resumed with the first 11 of the 'K3' class. They were numbered 1672-1696 and were an all-Leyland product with Metrovick motors and English Electric controllers. The only distinguishing mark from their 'K1' and 'K2' brothers was that their side lights were set in the front panels below the windscreen, rather than being side mounted.

During the Docklands pummelling, Poplar depot suffered some structural damage on 6 October, and in the many incidents in the days that followed, more trolleybuses had their bodies written off. On the 11th, No 1244 from Hackney was affected and No 1285 from Walthamstow was involved in an incident at Markhouse Road, where the crew were killed. On the 13th, No 861 from Wood Green and No 1001 from Holloway also had their bodies destroyed. On 2 November route 654 was disrupted, when blast damage affected the feeders at Anerley Hill. The most serious occurrence so far, however, was the bombing of Bexley depot on 7 November. Apart from the blast damage sustained by many vehicles, Nos 95, 406, 792 and 795 had their bodies completely destroyed. The following night No 1123 suffered the same fate when working from Stamford Hill. On the plus side, 11 more 'K3s' were delivered.

Vehicle shortages were now becoming a serious problem and, after negotiations with Bournemouth Corporation, 18 Sunbeam trolleybuses with Park Royal and English

Above:
Poplar depot received some blast damage on 6 October 1940, as can be seen here, as 'L3' No 1473 gingerly edges in from route 567. *London Transport*

Opposite:
The unluckiest trolleybus in the fleet must have been No 1001. Seen here on 14 October 1940 after a devastating air raid the night before, it was rebodied by Weymann in January 1942, and then destroyed again in July 1944. It was rebodied for a second time by East Lancs in December 1947.

Electric bodywork arrived on loan and were sent to Ilford depot to operate on routes 691 and 693. The last arrivals of the year were three more 'K3s' in December. The year closed with more bombings and, to illustrate the problem, a statement issued by the Board on 29/30 December underlines the typical state of operations after air raid damage: 'Trolleybus services are unable to reach their normal termini at London Docks, Minories, Moorgate and Holborn.' Twenty-four hours later, they reported: 'Trolleybus services are using the Holborn loop and Minories layby, and Gardiners Corner to the Minories, Commercial Road and Great Eastern Street have been reopened, with normal operations resumed in the Harrow Road.' The report went on to say, 'It is still not practicable for the trolleybus services to reach London Docks terminus, Moorgate terminus or to use the section of the Whitechapel Road between Cambridge Road and Commercial Street. Great Dover Street is closed, and there are a number of shorter sections of route where services are curtailed.'

After these raids, it was obvious that one of the most disruptive situations was unsafe buildings. Even after crews had repaired damage, some routes were refused permission to operate in the vicinity of any suspect structure and if the ARP didn't have enough men immediately available to demolish them, the route suspension could last for days rather than hours. The borough engineers and surveyors were approached regarding this problem and eventually permission was obtained for tramway breakdown crews to demolish unsafe buildings where they affected tram or trolleybus routes. Some 400 buildings were dealt with in this way, using special low-geared lorries equipped with a steel hawser, which was attached to the highest point of the structure. A very dangerous job!

By the end of 1940, route mileage had risen to 255, and 145 new vehicles had been received.

1941 arrived and it was declared that the war was now costing the country £11 million a day. The next deliveries, three in January and six in February, were of the 'P1' class. These were Leylands again but with Metro-Cammell bodies, Metrovick motors and English Electric controllers. They were numbered 1697-1721 and were initially allocated to Edmonton, Hammersmith and West Ham. Their bodies were basically similar to the 'L3s' but taller, owing to the fact that they were chassis-mounted.

The Luftwaffe, targeting the docks, hit West Ham depot on 9 March and as a result No 1492 was completely destroyed and Nos 621, 803 and 1247 all had their bodies destroyed. On the 19th, No 1587 had its body written off in a raid at Bow. Also during the month, Charterhouse Street was raided and the wires brought down, causing a wired-up diversion at Mount Pleasant to keep services

running. Six more 'P1s' were taken into stock in March and three more in April, while in that month bomb damage in Garratt Lane caused another wired diversion via Wilna Road. Vehicle deliveries were now almost drying up and the 'P1' received in May was the last one for three months.

Over 1,400 people were killed in the largest raid yet on 10 May, and in June came more bad news when Tobruk fell to the Germans. Back in London, changes to the routes in July were the new 569 from Silvertown station to Aldgate and the peak hours extension to Barking of the 565, both on the 23rd. During

August many cutbacks were made in administration and one that affected the Tram & Trolleybus Department was the standardisation of uniform. The Central Buses staff had blue piping to their uniforms, and the T&T men red, but from August blue was adopted as standard throughout. The saving grace was that the Trolley men kept their red cap badge.

Only two 'P1s' arrived that month, with three more following in September and the last one in October, completing the Board's current orders. Only the Kingsway subway tram routes now penetrated north of the river, and these and the South London routes figured in the extensive trolleybus scheme due to be introduced 'after the hostilities'.

During October Nos 1244 and 1285 re-emerged from Weymann's factory at Addlestone with new bodies after their war damage, and were given the suffix letter 'A' to their fleet

Opposite above:
On 7 November 1940 Bexley depot was hit in an air raid and suffered badly, four vehicles having their bodies completely destroyed. Two of them can be seen here on the morning after, Nos 795 and 406, both being rebodied by Weymann in November and December 1941 respectively. *London Transport*

Opposite below:
The morning after. 11 October 1940 at Leyton depot, and the damage to No 1244 is all too apparent. The chassis survived to be rebodied by Weymann in October 1941. *London Transport*

Left:
11 November 1940 at Leyton depot again. This time the casualty is 'K1' No 1277, having suffered blast damage. It was repaired by the Board in its own workshops. *London Transport*

numbers and reclassified 'K2A' and 'K1A' respectively. The Weymann rebuilds were similar in style to the 'M1' class but had a single skin roof which was distinctively ridged. On the 29th, new route 695 was introduced between Chadwell Heath and Bow Church.

Weymann delivered two more rebodied vehicles in November, Nos 792A and 795A (class 'H1A') and during the month some very strange new arrivals began to appear. Forty-three trolleybuses intended for delivery to operators in South Africa were diverted to London by order of the Ministry of Supply, due to the very high risks involved in shipping goods abroad. The vehicles were all 8ft wide and therefore exceeded the legal permitted width, but special permission was obtained for them to operate in the less crowded Ilford area, where they spent their entire working lives. They were classified 'SA1' Nos 1722-1733, 'SA2' Nos 1734-1746 and 'SA3' Nos 1747-1764. The 'SA1s' and 'SA2s' had Leyland chassis, and the 'SA3s' were based on the AEC 664T. 'SA1s' had GEC motors and controllers, the 'SA2s' Metrovick motors and controllers, and the 'SA3s' had English Electric equipment. All had bodywork by Metro-Cammell and had front sliding doors, which were panelled over in London. The destination boxes were all non-standard to London, and the top halves of the windows were fitted with darkened glass, to guard against the South African sun. They were built with all windows opening but half of these were locked by LT. No 1722, the first of these, came into stock in November followed by another four 'SA1s' in December.

Also in the last month of 1941 Weymann delivered rebodied Nos 1123A and 1247A, classified 'K1A' and 'K2A', along with No 406A, a 'D2A'. During November, nine of the Bournemouth Sunbeams went home as a

result of the new deliveries. Vehicle intake for the year was just 30.

January 1942 arrived and with it people were able to tune in their radio and listen to the new programme *Desert Island Discs*. In London, six standing passengers were now allowed on the lower deck of 611s descending Highgate Hill, No 1001A came home, rebuilt as a 'J2A' from Weymann, and four more 'SA1s' arrived. The following months saw more rebuilds come from the Addlestone factory: 'N1A' No 1587 in February, 'H1As' Nos 803A and 861A, 'K1A' No 1128A in March and Nos 95A, 107A and 'E2A' No 621A in April. Nos 95A and 107A had previously been short-wheelbase 'B' class 60-seaters but on rebodying had their chassis lengthened to the standard LT design and were reclassified 'D2A'.

The South African vehicles continued to trickle into stock: three 'SA1s' in February, two 'SA2s' in March and three in April. Weymann's last rebuild arrived in June in the shape of 'N1A' No 1565A, and the fleet was looking a bit healthier again with further 'SAs' arriving four 'SA2s' and two 'SA3s' coming in June, three more 'SA2s' in July and another in August.

London said farewell to the rest of the Bournemouth trolleybuses in September, as they continued their travels, this time to Newcastle. Another two 'SA3s' were taken into Ilford depot that month. The depot's clearout of 'E1s' went largely to West Ham and

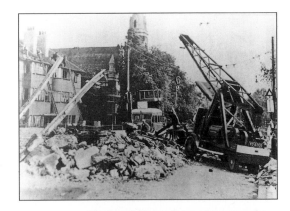

Above:
In December 1940 London Transport borrowed some Sunbeam trolleybuses from Bournemouth Corporation to cover for the shortages due to the hostilities. No 79, seen here on the 691, had bodywork by English Electric, was new in 1934, and was one of nine sent on to Newcastle in September 1942. *Omnibus Society*

Above left:
Maintenance crews had to work very hard to keep the services going during the Blitz and scenes such as this were all too common. An unidentified tower wagon is aided by No 353R, a 1926 4-ton crane.

Left:
The first of the Weymann-rebodied vehicles started to arrive in October 1941 and were all given fleet numbers with the suffix letter 'A'. No 1587A came in February 1942, and is caught on camera here at Hampton Court on the 667 in postwar years.
C. Carter

Walthamstow, where war-damaged vehicles
needed replacement. A solitary 'SA3' came in
October, and on the 31st new schedules were
introduced, with some trolleybuses from outer
depots being parked at inner depots during the
day, to save on mileage. On 11 November
another loss to the fleet occurred, although
this time not through enemy action. No 1365
burnt out in fog while in service on Seven
Sisters Road, as a result of overheating of the
resistance coil. The year ended with three
'SA3s' arriving in November and one in
December, bringing the total received for the
year to just 31, a far cry from the heady days
before the war.

1943 dawned, and the good news was that
Allied troops had recaptured Tripoli, but it was
not a very eventful year for the trolleybus fleet.
'SA3' deliveries were slowly completed, with
two in January, two in February and March,
one in May and the last two in June. During an
air raid in March, overhead was brought down
in Ilford and an Inspector travelling on a
trolleybus was killed in a machine gun attack.
On 3 May women between the ages of 18 and
45 were ordered into part-time employment
and the Board took many of these; also in May,
pride was boosted with the news of the

Dambusters raid. The last extension to the network took place on 14 July, when routes 696 and 698 were extended from the terminus at Woolwich Free Ferry, a short distance to a new turning loop at Parsons Hill, by the Odeon Cinema.

With vehicle deliveries now complete, the fleet weathered the raids without any major catastrophes. The *Air Raid Precautions Handbook*, which had been issued as long ago as 1938, stated, 'Members of staff who may be on duty in its depots or garages, will take cover in the repair pits, over which the vehicles will be standing.' In late 1943, the prototype 'M1' No 953 was completely burnt out in fog after a contactor fire, while in service from West Ham, and was scrapped the following January.

The night of 21/22 January 1944 saw another succession of raids on London, and in the following 12 weeks over 900 people lost their lives. Strikes occurred during April, over cuts in running times and working through lunch breaks, at Hackney, Poplar, West Ham, Leyton and Walthamstow on the 15th and 16th, Stamford Hill and Hackney on the 19th and Hounslow on the 22nd. Over at Bexley, route

694 finally bit the dust, after being previously discontinued on several occasions, when it was withdrawn on 28 May.

A new wave of terror hit Britain on 12 June, when the first 'V1' flying bomb arrived, bringing a new kind of warfare to the people. This new type of weapon brought chaos to the trolleybus system in the early hours of 29 June, when a direct hit decimated Bexley depot. Of the 84 vehicles present, 12 of them — Nos 99, 386/7, 394/8, 418, 428, 435, 448, 787, 791 and 812 were completely destroyed; 26 had their bodies completely written off — Nos 97/8, 385/9, 390/1/2/5/6/7, 402/5/7/9, and 415/19, 451, 766, 784/6, 790/4/9, 801/4/8 — and the rest were unserviceable due to blast damage. Despite this catastrophe a near normal service was provided the following evening with vehicles ferried in from all over the system, a tribute to the typical spirit shown throughout the war years, when people refused to be beaten.

Disruption moved south to Anerley Hill on 11 July, when four bays of overhead were brought down and the reverser at the foot of the hill was used to turn trolleybuses back to Sutton. A particularly tragic incident occurred on 27 July, when No 1387 in service at Dames Road, Wanstead Flats, received a direct hit. The firefighters' report states that 16 houses were also demolished and a total of 35 people lost their lives.

The month ended on another bad note when, on the 30th, West Ham's works and canteen were hit during another docks raid. No 364 was completely written off and 18 trolleybuses had their bodies destroyed — Nos 412, 430, 470, 578, 602, 623/6/9, 633/5, 641/3, 993, 1001A, 1007, 1385, 1543/5. No 1001A was extremely unlucky in having its second body destroyed. The English Electric chassisless No 1670 had its roof damaged and was subsequently reroofed by Weymann. The bad news continued into August, when No 575 had its body written off while in service at Hoe Street on the 16th. The summer of 1944 was frightening: the first 'V2' rocket descended and a further 500 were to follow in the period ending March 1945.

A diversion took place in Wandsworth for route 612 on 29 November, and at about that time 45 reconditioned chassis left London for

East Lancs and Northern Coachbuilders for new bodies. During the year J. C. Beadle of Dartford carried out rebuilding work on Nos 403, 406A and 1123A, and Fulwell works did likewise with No 797. Damage at Walthamstow depot in January 1945 resulted in No 378 being withdrawn and then selected for rebuilding in connection with the Pay-as-you-Board experiment. Charlton rebuilt No 401 in January and Nos 417 and 793 in February, while Fulwell works handled work on No 404.

The Allies' controversial bombing of Dresden took place in February, which many people saw as revenge for the rocket attacks on Britain. One such attack on Smithfield Market brought down the wires in Farringdon Road in March.

Former LUT No 61 was outshopped as a Pay-as-you-Board vehicle on route 604 in March. The conductor had a cash desk under the stairs and seats were moved on the nearside to allow circulation. The vehicle was also converted to full-width bulkhead and the conductor was provided with a periscope to view the upper deck. More rebuilds followed: Nos 426 and 788 from Charlton works in March and No 94 in April.

The news everyone had longed for finally came on 8 May 1945, when VE Day was proudly proclaimed. All other news was dwarfed by the celebrations and the tired nation breathed a heavy sigh of relief. During the conflict 181 LT staff had lost their lives on duty and 1,867 had been injured.

More war damage rebuilds continued to return to service. Beadles returned No 811 in June and No 807 in October and also dealt with Nos 393, 400 and 416. Charlton treated No 106 in June, No 427 in August and Nos 785 and 806 in October. No 393 was particularly unlucky, having to be rebuilt by Beadles and again by Charlton in December. The first of the East Lancs rebodied vehicles came into stock as

Opposite:
All types of vehicles were used at Bexley during the mopping up period after the flying bomb incident. 'M1' No 1549 is captured here at Abbey Wood on the 698.

Above:
Another helper at Bexley was 'P1' No 1720, a Leyland-bodied MCCW vehicle new in September 1941. It is working here on the 696 journey to Abbey Wood.

No 391B in September, followed by No 390B in October and Nos 392B and 409B in November, and No 407B in December. These vehicles were similar to the 'L' and 'M' types but with a higher central cream band, only one opening windscreen and a single ventilator over the offside screen.

Behind the scenes, the Board had received quotations during September for new vehicles as planned replacements for the ageing former LUT fleet. No 61 was withdrawn from the Pay-as-you-Board experiment in October and on 21 November the winter schedules were welcomed, with most wartime restrictions being cancelled. No 378 emerged in December to take its place in the PAYB experiments. Again a cash desk was provided, situated under the stairs, and the platform was rebuilt with a step and folding doors. An emergency door was fitted in the rear wall, and the vehicle worked route 604 from Fulwell.

The year culminated with the receipt of the first Northern Coachbuilders rebody, when No 402C was delivered. They were not unlike the 'N1s' in appearance, although they were of composite construction and not metal framed. They had deeper rainshields and, like the East Lancs product, had a fixed nearside screen and single offside screen ventilator.

So the war was over and peace had begun, but it was to be an uphill struggle for London's trolleybus fleet and the high points were to be very few.

Right:
30 July 1944 was another bad day for the network, when West Ham's works and canteen were hit. One trolleybus was completely destroyed and 18 had their bodies written off. No 792A on the left had a near miss, having been rebodied once after damage at Bexley in 1940. The photograph was taken on 2 August. *London Transport*

The demand for trams and trolleybuses was some 9% greater in 1946 than in 1939 but resources were not to hand in those austere times, and although costs had increased considerably since before the war, only one fares increase had been implemented, in 1940. The South London tram conversions now seemed remote, especially when the Board announced that all remaining trams were to enter a renovation scheme, carried out by Charlton works and Purley depot.

Rebodied vehicles back from Northern Coachbuilders in January were Nos 385C, 397C and 430C. In February the all-night services were restored to prewar levels, and NCB delivered No 97C, whose chassis had been lengthened to accommodate a 70-seat body and was therefore reclassified 'D2C'. No 389C also arrived in this month, followed in March by No 98C, another reclassified 'D2C'. East Lancs now responded with Nos 405B, 412B and 451B in March and No 395B in April.

The March schedules restored more evening and late journeys lost in the war, as did the schedules announced for April. No 378's participation in the Pay-as-you-Board experiment came to an end in March and its doors were removed before re-entering service. The rest of the 1946 rebodied trolleybus returns were as follows: East Lancs — Nos 470B in June, 790B, 801B in August,

CHAPTER 6
1946
AND AFTER

Below:
Rebodied vehicles from Northern Coachbuilders started to arrive back in the capital in December 1945. 'D2' No 430 had been damaged at West Ham Works in July 1944, and its new body can be seen here at the NCB works, prior to being sent on the long journey south to London.
Newcastle City Libraries and Arts

804B in September, 766B in October: NCB — Nos 575C, 578C, 602C and 623C in May, 626C and 635C in June, 633C in July, 419C in August, 629C, 641C and 643C in September. On 6 June the Board received a report from the Development and Research Department recommending what many had advocated for some time: that the remaining trams should be replaced by diesel buses, not trolleybuses. The report was studied and subsequently agreed by the Board and eventually approved by the Ministry of Transport. The announcement was made public in November.

On 8 June Central London was closed for the Victory Celebrations and processions took place from various points around the capital, all converging on the centre. As a result, trolleybuses turned at the nearest loops to Kingsland Road, Mile End, Mare Street, Angel and Commercial Road.

Of some significance was the issue of the first Tram & Trolleybus map since 1940, although its similarity to the Underground style of straight lines of no geographical consequence did not win it many friends. December saw the first withdrawal among the former London United vehicles, when Diddler

Opposite above:
The East Lancs rebodied trolleybuses started to appear from September 1945. This posed view at Hampton Court shows No 801B in August 1946, looking very smart and ready for service. It had been one of the unlucky vehicles at Bexley on the night of 29 June 1944, when a flying bomb struck.
London Transport

Opposite below:
'C3' No 378 had suffered war damage at Walthamstow depot in January 1945 and was rebuilt as a Pay-as-you-Board bus. It was fitted with a pay desk for the conductor under the stairs, and folding doors. An emergency exit door was fitted at the rear of the bus. This view is at Fulwell after the experiment had ended.

Above:
In January 1947 'B1' Nos 66, 70 & 88 were fitted with transmitters to control radio operated points. The aerials were easily recognisable on the roof, as can be seen here on No 88, pictured at Norwood Junction in later years. *G. E. Baddeley*

No 47 was withdrawn. It was scrapped at Fulwell in December 1948.

A decision was taken during 1946 to adopt the Johnston style of script on trolleybus blinds and a batch was made for Hounslow late in the year. They were manufactured by the same, much cheaper, method as the bus blinds, being paper on cotton rather than silk screen printed on cloth. These had blue lettering on a black background. Trolleybuses had always used blue bulbs in their destination boxes but this was later phased out as the supply of the bulbs became difficult. 1946 was also the year in which the night services received route numbers for the first time, in June.

1947 dawned and people read in their newspapers that the National Coal Board had come into existence, and that they now owned the mines. To the south of the capital, at Sutton, an experiment took place in January when three vehicles, Nos 66, 70 and 88, were fitted with an electric induction device operated by a switch in the cab, to operate points at West Croydon. It did not bear fruit, however, and was not expanded on. More rebodied buses continued to trickle into stock throughout the year from East Lancs; Nos 786B, 799B and 808B in January, 784B in February, 794B in April and 993B and 1001B in December, No 1001 having had its second body destroyed in July 1944.

1947 is renowned for its harsh winter, 29 January being the coldest on record for 20 years. Over 120 trolleybuses had motors damaged by snow during this period and Charlton works presumably had much reconditioning to carry out. To give some idea of the affluence trolleybus staff enjoyed, the *LT News* of 27 June announced that the new weekly rate of pay agreed with the TGWU was 117s 6d after 2 years' service (£5.87½). Staff in training could expect 10s 10d (54p) per day, although some women were only entitled to 9s 9d (49p) per day.

On 1 January 1948 the old LPTB was swept away and replaced by the London Transport Executive, part of the British Transport Commission. However, this would have little effect on the trolleybus system, as its future, or lack of it, had already been settled by its predecessor. The delivery of the East Lancs vehicles finally came to an end after Nos 1007B and 1385B arrived in January, 1545B in March and 1543B in April. No 1385B was the odd one out, being originally a chassisless vehicle; a new standard AEC 664T chassis-frame was sent to the factory and the resulting vehicle was reclassified 'N1B'. This chassis was presumably a spare, as the 664T was out of production at this time.

Also in January, an 8ft-wide BUT trolleybus destined for Johannesburg was borrowed and tried in the Hampton Court area, to judge whether the wider buses would be suited to the district. This all tied in with the quotations received back in September 1945, when prices were sought for new vehicles to replace the old London United fleet. The specification originally laid down had been amended in several ways, most significant being that the vehicle would be 8ft wide and of five-bay construction rather than the previous standard of six. The first order was for 77, presumably to replace the 60 Diddlers and the 17 vehicles lost in the war.

The first five of the new 'Q1' class arrived in February 1948. The class was numbered 1765-1841 and had chassis by British United Traction, a pooling of trolleybus resources by AEC and Leyland, and bodywork by Metro-Cammell. English Electric built the controllers and Metrovick supplied the floodproof motors. No 1841 was the odd one out, in that it was supplied with Metrovick automatic acceleration equipment, which incidentally did not prove very popular with drivers. Nos 1838-1840 were also fitted with automatic acceleration equipment by English Electric, but were soon converted to normal control. The class was fitted with a visual and audible low pressure alarm, to warn the driver if the air pressure dropped below 50psi and was not restored. Control equipment had been tried in service for 12 months prior to fitting to the new vehicles.

A demonstration run took place prior to service beginning, with guests including local mayors, Ministry of Transport officials, police representatives and people from BUT, English Electric, MCW, Metropolitan Vickers and, of course, London Transport. The 'Q1s' were all allocated to Fulwell depot and were instantly liked by staff and public alike for their ride qualities. They must have seemed light years ahead of the Diddlers which they replaced. The chassis were initially assembled at Leyland's factory at Ham in Surrey, but the operation was later transferred to AEC at Southall, when Leyland sold the site at Ham in 1948. Interestingly, Chiswick produced experimental blinds for these vehicles, blue

Opposite above:
The death knell for the Diddlers was sounded in February 1948, when the first of the 'Q1' class vehicles were delivered. Two had been withdrawn prior to this but between September and the following June large numbers of the class were replaced. No 49, seen here in the February 1948 snow at Hampton Court, lasted until June 1949. *Alan Cross*

Opposite below:
Five 'Q1s' were delivered in February 1948, and No 1779, complete with chalked number plate, is seen on the tilt test before delivery. The first batch of 77 were all in stock by March 1949.

lettering on black as in some of the earlier products, but these did not find favour and were soon replaced.

A curious accident occurred on 9 February, when a light aeroplane overshot the runway at Hendon and struck trolleybus No 215, which was working the 645 at Burnt Oak. Fortunately, only 10 passengers were on board and no one was seriously hurt. On 1 March 'Q1s' entered service on route 604, and deliveries continued with four in March, three in April, 10 in May, 11 in June, 13 in July, eight in August, 10 in September, two each in October and November, and four in December.

Events during the year varied. The extension of the Central Line to Hainault in May affected loadings on route 661 and as a result five vehicles were cut from the schedule. The Olympic Games came to Britain on 29 July and the Tram & Trolleybus Department provided special services from Paddington to Wembley and Scrubs Lane to Wembley. From 10 November the 'SA' class trolleybuses began appearing beyond their normal area of work, being seen as far afield as Bow Church, when the new schedules shared working on route 695 between Bow and Ilford. An interesting fact is that twice as many people were compensated for tramway accidents than

trolleybus accidents during the year, despite the fact that there were twice as many trolleybuses as trams.

The new year of 1949 was greeted with a strike on 1 January, with claims for time and a half for Saturday afternoon work. The 'Q1' deliveries were completed, with three in January, one in February and one in March. On 17 April Sunday journeys which had operated between Wood Green and Liverpool Street showing 649 were renumbered 649A,

and thus Stamford Hill became the only depot operating a route with a suffix letter.

By this time, the Weymann rebodied vehicles were showing distinct signs of distress, a common feature in war-built vehicles, due mainly to the unseasoned timber used in their construction. Mann-Egerton at Norwich were contacted and a rebuilding programme was drawn up. The Norfolk-based company had previously performed similar tasks for the bus fleet. New timbers were installed, as well as new staircases, all of which made the vehicle a real heavyweight at over 9ton 14cwt.

Back in the capital, morning peak journeys on route 655 were extended to Acton Vale, Bromyard Avenue, on 8 June, making it the longest trolleybus route on the system, a title previously held by the 630. June was a bad month for the Diddlers, 24 being withdrawn, although after withdrawal in September, No 1 was retained for preservation. The last of these former LUT vehicles finished service on 29 September.

July 1950 proved to be a significant month

for the Tram & Trolleybus Department. It had always been operated as a separate entity from the Central Buses, but that month the two were merged under the banner of Central Road Services and, for many, the writing was on the wall.

Up to this point, trolleybuses had carried only running number plates on their sides, but now all depots were given code letters to fall into line with their bus counterparts, and as some depots had the same name as local bus garages, six were renamed. Hackney became Clapton, Hendon became Colindale, Holloway was to be known as Highgate, Hounslow became Isleworth, Leyton changed to Lea Bridge and finally Sutton was renamed Carshalton. This merging of departments meant the end of the old institution of the Workman's ticket, and the 'Workman' rear blind display operating up to 8am was discontinued.

Operation Tramaway was under way in South London, and when on 30 September 1950 the tram routes out of Wandsworth were withdrawn, the opportunity was seized to remove electric traction altogether from the depot . The withdrawal of route 612 was the first loss of route miles that the system had suffered, and the small involvement Wandsworth had in the 630 was transferred to Hammersmith.

Around 1950, 'Q1' No 1768 made a trip taking in Highgate Hill and Finchley Road, loaded with special equipment for

Above:
During 1950 what appears to have been a 'hush hush' trip was made using 'Q1' No 1768. It is known to have traversed Highgate Hill, and photographs exist of it near Finchley depot and on the way to Barnet. Here it is pulling out of Willifield Way on batteries, after reversing in. The location is just south of the North Circular Road, on Finchley Road. *Quadrant Picture Library*

Opposite:
Approaching the Nags Head junction, a real headache for any trolleybus trainee driver. 'J3' No 1050 was fitted with coasting and runback brakes for use on the 611 on Highgate Hill. It is 11 April 1951 but, judging by the presence of heavy coats, spring has not quite arrived yet.
London Transport

experimental trials, of which very little has come to light, but this was one of only two to stray from their usual sphere of operations, apart from an enthusiasts' tour.

The year came to an end and the British public had at last seen the end of soap rationing in September, and were singing a new song called 'I've got a lovely bunch of coconuts'.

The last Diddlers were withdrawn in January 1951, after serving for a brief spell as trainers, leaving No 61 as the last London United link, that vehicle surviving until September. The first 'B2' was withdrawn in December and, due to the bad condition of the class, nearly all had been withdrawn before the end of 1952.

The second batch of 'Q1s' arrived in 1952, the first nine coming from Birmingham in May. These were identical to the first batch, apart from the siting of the batteries, which were under the offside long seat rather than under the stairs as on the earlier batch. They

were to be numbered 1842-1891 and arrived throughout the year: three in June, one in July, six in August, 11 in September, six in November and the final 14 in December. No 1891 differed in that it was fitted when new with English Electric automatic acceleration, although, like Nos 1838-40 before, it was soon converted to conventional control. On the other side of the coin, the LPTB prototypes were withdrawn during the year, No 63 coming off in June and No 62 in October.

The biggest event during the year, however, was the end of London's trams, finally biting the dust on 5 July and replaced by the diesel bus. Trolleybus routes now began to appear on the Central Bus Map. The year will be remembered by many as a particularly tragic one: the King died in February, 31 were killed in floods in August, 28 were killed at the Farnborough Air Show, 112 in the Harrow train crash and nearly 4,000 died as a result of the London smog. Amid all this despair, Charlton works ceased to make blinds, the last

sets going to Edmonton depot.

1952 marked the peak in London's trolleybus fleet size: 1,811 were in stock during that year, then from 1953 the figure fell continuously. January 1953 came and with it 13 'D3' class vehicles were withdrawn and the new 'Q1s' began to appear on route 607 from Hanwell. They were banned from route 655, although No 1847 is known to have worked it on one occasion. The new Gibson ticket machines made their first appearance on the trolleybus scene in April, when they were used at Isleworth. Fulwell got them in August and eventually all depots were converted, finishing in the east by 1957. The nation settled down on 2 June 1953 to listen to (or, if you were more affluent, to watch) the Coronation of Queen Elizabeth II. As a point of interest, many trolleybuses operated on Christmas Day during the 1950s and, as an example, 826 were scheduled to work on Christmas Day 1953.

In January 1954 the former Pay-as-you-Board trolleybus No 378 was finally withdrawn for scrap. By far the most significant item of interest during the year was the announcement on 28 April that the trolleybus fleet would be replaced by buses, commencing in January 1958. It was planned to leave the services operated by Fulwell and Isleworth until a later date, to allow the newer, postwar 'Q1s' operating there to fulfil their life expectancy.

1955 was another bad year for the fleet; passenger receipts continued to fall and as a result, mass withdrawals took place, starting in March when 51 'C' types, the five 'B3s', seven 'E3s' and two 'F1s' came off. Joining them were the experimentals Nos 754 and 1379. More followed in May and June, as more vehicles became surplus to requirements, including experimental vehicles Nos 1670 and 1671.

A most interesting sale took place in May 1956, when five 'C1s' were sold to Georgetown Municipal Transport in Penang, Malaya. No 175 became their No 22 and was sent out in

Top:
May 1952 saw the first arrivals of the second batch of 'Q1s'. Apart from the battery positioning, they were to the same specification as their predecessors, and the batch of 50 vehicles was in stock by the end of the year. No 1874 was delivered in November and was sent to Isleworth for the 657. *Alan Cross*

Above:
Looking very presentable at Barking is 'SA2' No 1744, which shares the stand with 'SA3' No 1757 on route 693. Note the panelled-over front sliding doors.

Opposite above:
Considerable numbers of trolleybuses could be seen operating on Christmas Day in the 1950s. One curious working concerned Carshalton, which operated vehicles as extras on the 630 between West Croydon and Mitcham. They did not carry a route number, as can be seen here, as 'B1' No 490 stands at West Croydon awaiting custom.

Opposite below:
In May 1956, five 'C1' trolleybuses were sold to Georgetown Municipal Transport in Malaya. The vehicles, Nos 138, 142, 148, 175 and 183, retained their open platforms but were fitted with additional opening windows and trafficators. No 20, formerly LT No 142, is shown here.

May, the other four — Nos 138, 142, 148 and 183 — following in June, becoming Nos 24, 20, 21 and 23 in the Penang fleet. They retained their open platforms but were fitted with additional opening windows and trafficators.

During 1956 'Q1' No 1856 was badly damaged in an accident and was sent to Charlton works for repairs. On completion, the vehicle was towed in August to the Bexleyheath area wires to be tested and must have been a rare treat for any enthusiast who came in contact with it. Another vehicle to leave Charlton, but for a completely different reason, was No 1662, which was burnt out there in August while in for overhaul, and was officially withdrawn in November.

On 16 October route 565 was withdrawn as part of a package of economies announced, and in December orders were placed with Park Royal and AEC for the new Routemaster buses destined to replace the trolleybus. More 'C' and 'D' classes were withdrawn during the year, along with more 'E3s', but things

stabilised in 1957 when only 10 vehicles were taken out of service, including some of the Weymann-rebodied trolleybuses.

There was a sign that the onward march of the motorbus was imminent when, in March 1958, work began at Bexleyheath and Carshalton Depots on adapting the premises for the next generation. Other depots followed during that year: Poplar in May, Clapton in June and Bow in September. 1958 saw more withdrawals from the older classes but the event that was to cast a shadow over the year was the strike that crippled London between 5 May and 21 June. The strike is well documented and its effect on passenger loadings was irreversible.

The last new section of overhead on the system came into use in July 1958 when, as part of the new traffic management scheme at Hammersmith, the bus station at Butterwick was opened. That September, due to flood damage, Carshalton was short of vehicles for the 654, and as a result three 'J3s' (Nos 1049-51) were borrowed from Highgate for about two weeks, the only known occasion when 70-seaters worked this route.

No sooner had 1959 dawned than on 6 January service cuts brought about the withdrawal of routes 664, 683 and 695. From then on it was downhill all the way. On 3 March the trolleybus conversion scheme began, when Bexleyheath and Carshalton lost their stocks of trolleybuses and routes 696, 698 and 654 were replaced by RT buses operating the new routes. Stage two

followed on soon afterwards on 14 April, when Clapton changed over to RTL operation and Lea Bridge closed its doors completely, on the withdrawal of routes 555, 581 and 677. Hopes that the new Routemasters would be ready for stage three faded, and RT family buses were again used on 18 August when Bow and Ilford were converted, losing routes 661, 663, 691 and 693. Ilford closed its doors for the last time.

Rumours circulated that the 'SA' class vehicles had found an overseas buyer and

Opposite above:
Service cuts due to lack of patronage were inevitable after the 1958 bus strike, and the trolleybus network was not exempt. Three routes were withdrawn on 6 January 1959, the 664, 683 and 695. 'N1' No 1639 from Bow depot is seen here at Bow Church, about to terminate and return to Chadwell Heath. It has a non-standard front grille, with six sets of louvres instead of the usual three or two.
Norman Rayfield, LCC Tramways Trust

Opposite below:
The first stage of the conversion scheme took place on 3 March 1959, when the isolated Bexleyheath and Carshalton routes were withdrawn. No 391B, an East Lancs rebodied vehicle, was originally at Bexleyheath, where the 1944 flying bomb incident destroyed its first body. Years later, it can be seen leaving the stand at Parsons Hill, Woolwich, bound for Bexleyheath on the 698. *Norman Rayfield, LCC Tramways Trust*

indeed there may have been some truth in this, as they were not handed over to Cohens until January/February 1960. During September, 'C2' No 260 was presented to the Museum of Transport at Clapham.

Routemasters finally came onto the scene on 10 November at stage four, when routes 567, 569 and 665 became history and Poplar became a bus garage. West Ham on the other hand started a six month period when it would operate both types of vehicle. November was also the month when the 'C' class buses sold to Malaya were withdrawn.

Stage five on 2 February 1960 involved Walthamstow and West Ham. Routes 557, 669, 685, 689 and 690 bit the dust, although both depots continued to operate trolleybuses until stage six on 26 April, when they both finally

Above:
It is the eve of 14/15 April 1959 and 'K2' No 1327 is about to be the last trolleybus to come home at Lea Bridge depot. A rather wooden line-up of employees, and what appears to be two posed bus enthusiasts, survey the scene. It will be very different tomorrow; the depot will be closed and the staff transferred elsewhere. *London Transport*

Above left:
In August 1959 Bow and Ilford lost their trolleybuses and Ilford closed for good. 'SA3' No 1757 on route 691 has turned short at Newbury Park and is leaving the stand in Birkbeck Road, bound for Barking. *Brian Speller*

Above:
Bow routes 661 and 663 were replaced by RTL buses in April 1959. 'N1' No 1615 waits over at Aldgate, with 'L3' No 1439 waiting behind on the 567. It too will go before the year is out. Both trollies will live to fight another day, however, as they will be transferred elsewhere. *Norman Rayfield, LCC Tramways Trust*

Right:
Poplar depot had its fleet swept away in November 1959 and became the first to use the new Routemaster bus for its intended purpose. East End trunk route 665 between Barking and Bloomsbury was one casualty, and 'L3' No 1481, typical of the vehicles that worked the route, is seen here.

Below right:
Route 623 bade farewell on 26 April 1960 after over 24 years' service. No 892 was an 'H1' delivered in June 1938, and never saw service after this conversion. The former tramway offices on the right are all that now remain of the Walthamstow depot site. *Omnibus Society*

Bottom right:
Also withdrawn on 26 April 1960 were Docklands routes 687 and 697. Walthamstow's 'H1' No 765 is ahead of West Ham's 'E1' No 587 at the docks terminus in August 1959. *Norman Rayfield, LCC Tramways Trust*

Left:
'P1s' were a common sight on the Hammersmith routes; No 1705 tours the Broadway at Hammersmith on a run-in. It survived until April 1961. *Brian Speller*

Below left:
Docks route 699 had been jointly operated by West Ham and Walthamstow since its inception in June 1936. It lasted until April 1960. At Greengate is 'M1' No 1541, which was transferred and finally withdrawn in April 1961. *C. Carter*

Below:
In November 1960 the conversion swung over to Hanwell, which lost its two routes, the 607 and 655. The 'F1' Leylands had ruled the roost here, with the exception of a few 'Q1s' in later years, and one of their number, No 751, is shown here turning short on the 607 at Southall, Delamere Road. *Pamlin Prints*

succumbed to the motorbus. On this date the 623, 625, 687, 697 and 699 were withdrawn, Wood Green losing its share of the 625 on the same date.

Stage seven came on 19 July 1960, when Hammersmith closed its doors to operations on conversion of routes 626, 628 and 630. Highgate featured too, losing just the 611. In October 'H1' No 796 was shipped to France for display in the Paris Transport Museum, where it remains in 'as withdrawn' condition.

On 8 November stage eight featured just Hanwell's routes, 607 and 655, and at last Uxbridge Road lost its electric transport. With this conversion began the mass withdrawals of the 'Q1' class. This followed deals struck with various Spanish operators to purchase 125 of the class, the odd ones being the non-standard Nos 1841 and 1768, which had been earmarked for the museum. Hanwell's batch were delicensed and sent to Fulwell for a while, prior to being moved to Poplar as a stepping stone to shipment from the nearby

docks. The withdrawals continued from January 1961 onwards and shipping out began in February. All had left British shores before the end of the year and, at around £500 each, they would prove to be a bargain buy.

On 31 January 1961 Highgate starred, as routes 513/613, 517/617, 615, 639 and 653 became casualties of stage nine. The trend towards preservation continued, when in March 'Q1' No 1768 was indeed presented to the Museum of Transport at Clapham. Highgate clung on to its last trolleybuses until stage 10 on 25 April, when it joined Edmonton and Wood Green as routes 627, 629, 659 and 679 came to an end, leaving the latter two depots operating both buses and trolleybuses side by side. Highgate lost its small Sunday allocation for route 609 at this time, and operated Routemasters with 609 blinds alongside Finchley's trolleybuses until the route was withdrawn.

Clapham's collection was enlarged further in May 1961, when No 1253 became the fourth

to enter the ranks of preservation. Stamford Hill and Edmonton were cleared of trolleybuses at stage 11 on 18 July, after routes 543/643, 647 and 649 were withdrawn. The 649A, being a Sunday-only route, finished on 16 July. A strange sight would have greeted any member of the public at Shepherds Bush during August, when No 1201 appeared at Welham Auto Services car lot, painted white and parked as a storeroom against a wall, the side nearest the wall still bearing LT livery. This vehicle finally ended up in preservation with the London Trolleybus Preservation Society (LTPS) in 1968, and awaits restoration at Sandtoft.

Back to the conversions, and stage 12 came on 7 November, when Wood Green lost its last trolleybuses and Finchley its first few, as routes 521/621, 609 and 641 disappeared. The end was now in sight as 'snowy' stage 13, as it became known, arrived in freezing conditions on 2 January 1962. The appalling weather saw off the 645, 660, 662 and 666, with Finchley and Stonebridge becoming bus garages and Colindale closing its doors for good.

The final vehicle to depart for preservation, in April of that year, was No 1348, which left for Ireland and the Transport Museum Society,

Opposite:
January 1961, and the Holborn routes were affected. 'K1' No 1105 leads 'L1' No 1366 at Chancery Lane on routes 613 and 617 in 1960. The main rear end difference between these two classes can be seen here, as the 'K' classes had the lower doorway. *John Glover*

Above:
A rear study at King's Cross, with 'M1' No 1542 on the 513. This trolleybus was officially withdrawn in April 1961, just three months after the route disappeared. *David Packer*

Above right:
Also finishing in January 1961 was the 615 from Highgate. 'B3' No 488, one of the short-wheelbase 60-seaters, is seen here at Parliament Hill Fields. Note the side lights positioned in the cream band between decks. *C. Carter*

where unfortunately it spent many years in the open deteriorating, though it is now under cover.

The culmination of the £10.5 million conversion scheme came on 8 May 1962, when Fulwell became a garage and Isleworth closed. Routes 601-5, 657 and 667 were the last to go. This stage is covered elsewhere in this book.

And so it was all over. In a space of just over three years, the system had been dismantled. The replacement bus route numbers were kept as familiar as possible for the travelling public; indeed, night bus routes, which were numbered in the 200 series, were altered to receive an 'N' prefix, replacing the '2' and releasing numbers for trolleybus replacement routes. Many routes introduced at the time are still familiar today, such as the 96, 207, 266, 279 etc, although some have been replaced by a hotchpotch of subsequent route alterations. As for the trolleybuses themselves, some led a rather charmed life as the conversion scheme progressed generally anticlockwise from the east to the southwest. The older classes left for the scrapyard, but the more recent and serviceable vehicles, with some exceptions, moved on. Trusty 'K1', 'K2', 'L3', 'N1' and 'N2' vehicles found themselves ferried from depot to depot, finding themselves in often unfamiliar surroundings. 'K1s' and 'K2s', after leaving Walthamstow, Lea Bridge and Clapton, for example, travelled on to Stamford Hill, Edmonton, Wood Green and finally Isleworth, and 'L3s', after leaving their home territory in the East End, ended up working at Finchley, Stonebridge and Fulwell. Their fellow East Enders, the 'N1s' and 'N2s', travelled on to Stonebridge and Colindale. Many other

Above:
In July 1961 Edmonton was involved, and the 649 became history. 'K2' No 1315 is seen here against a very threatening sky, at one of the most famous landmarks on the system, 'Trolley Bus Café', at Tramway Avenue.

Opposite above:
July 1961 saw the end of route 647 between Stamford Hill and London Docks. Stamford Hill depot had operated the route since it started in February 1939, and 'K2' No 1216 is typical of the stock used on this service.

Opposite below:
The 609 was converted to buses in November 1961, using the first of the then experimental RML class on new route 104. Seen here leaving Finchley depot to work to Barnet is 'L3' No 1529, which was one of five of the class to be fitted with sliding windows rather than the usual half-drop. Nos 1471, 1472, 1527 and 1528 were the others.

vehicles of older manufacture, such as the 'F1's, which were in mainly excellent condition, could have carried on too but were scrapped mainly because of their age.

So, the activities of standing at junctions watching convoys of trolleybuses glide by and waiting by tight curves hoping for a dewirement were no more. The crews and public alike had enjoyed the trolleybuses. They were popular and still generally in good order when they were withdrawn. The crews and the maintenance staff always seemed to remain separate from the motorbus staff, retaining an independence that they had enjoyed just over a decade earlier when they shared a department with the tramways

A few vehicles have survived, however. No 260, originally earmarked for Clapham but replaced by No 1253, was sold to Cohens for scrap in July but was rescued at the eleventh hour. It now resides at Carlton Colville, where it still operates alongside No 1521, the last of all, which was saved by Cohens after stage 14. 'Q1' No 1768 makes the occasional visit and also operates. As a postscript to 'Q1' excursions in Spain, No 1812 was rescued after withdrawal from the Santander-Astillero system in November 1974, and was finally purchased in May 1977 and shipped back home in June of that year. It currently awaits restoration at Sandtoft. Strictly for the record, the last ex-London vehicle of all to operate in Spain was No 1815, in January 1979 in La Coruna. Reports as late as September 1995 suggest that in all, six 'Q1s' still exist in Spain, Nos 1836, 1837 and 1839 all in preservation in the Zaragoza area, and Nos 1818, 1834 and 1838 all sold to individuals for various other purposes. It is particularly interesting to note that all of those surviving 'Q1s' are from the first batch and all

are in the Zaragoza area.

And so the demise of the system was complete. Once the biggest system in the world, at its height operating 1,811 vehicles in 1952, and in 1950 its maximum of 65 routes out of 21 depots, it was efficient and effective. Many routes operated 3min frequencies, and complex junctions, such as the one at the Nags Head, were a wonder to behold, with nearly 300 vehicles per hour in morning peaks in the early 1950s. One can suppose that perhaps they were only ever regarded as a temporary replacement for the tram and a means to utilise the expensive infrastructure already in existence, and it is good to fantasize on what would have happened in South London, had war not intervened. In the end the motorbus had won. 'More flexible,' they said; they didn't, of course, say it was noisier and dirtier; it wasn't so important then, but it is more significant now.

The last entry in the diary is Tuesday 8 May 1962. To set the scene, 'Wonderful Land' by the Shadows was top of the pops, people were arguing about the hanging of James Hanratty the previous month and Britain had just had its first satellite launched from Cape Canaveral.

It was a lovely sunny morning and I had managed to talk my parents into letting me have the day off school for this vitally important day in my life. My usual journey to trolleybus territory from Blackheath was a 53 to New Cross, a 36 to the Oval and a 155 to Wimbledon. All through the journey I contemplated the day before me. Could this really be the last day that I would ride on a London trolleybus? They said it would be, but it was hard to believe.

Approaching Wimbledon Town Hall, I always had this feeling of expectancy, waiting to glimpse the overhead and hoping a trolleybus would be on the stand. No problem, a 604 was there waiting, and on I got. The ride from there to Kingston was always enjoyable, especially the Raynes Park section, but why

the hell didn't I get off and photograph it there? Armed with my Ilford Sporti and I think three rolls of film, because that was all my pocket money savings would stretch to, I planned my campaign.

We passed the Malden turning circle and headed for Norbiton, where we joined the 603 wires for Kingston. I got off here and, with my trusty camera and the sun streaming down, I

CHAPTER 7
THE LAST DAY

Below:
Not quite the last day, but Saturday 5 May 1962. This is a wonderful shot of two 'L3s' at James Road, Kingston. No 1413 on the left has turned short and waits to resume on the 605, while No 1433 prepares to pass on the 601 on its way to Twickenham.
Leslie Sandler

froze several of those heady moments, all the time not believing that this was the end.

After walking around the town and visiting the bus station, I pointed the camera at a Twickenham-bound 601, when an old lady stopped and said, 'Shouldn't you be taking that one?' and she pointed back behind me. I turned, and to my absolute amazement, coming towards me was Diddler No 1, in a procession, followed by a gleaming No 1521. I hurriedly took a couple of shots and she was gone, to travel to Richmond Park loop, so I overheard, via the 602, and ending up at the bus station. Everybody rushed over the road to await her arrival. It was the first time I had

ever seen her and I had no idea she was to be on the road that day. We were not so well informed in those days.

When she eventually arrived, it was difficult to get a clear view without other people in the way, but I managed a couple of shots. Now as the towing lorry was being hitched to tow her back to the Museum at Clapham, horror struck. My camera had jammed. The shutter wouldn't operate, and I was desperate; I had a half-exposed film inside and I was completely snookered. When stuck in a tight corner, there's only one person who can normally help you out and that's good old Mum. With all the possible cheek I could muster, I telephoned her with an SOS. This was a desperately urgent situation and a plea for help, as this day would never come again. I needed my standby camera, won at bingo, the trusty Coronet. It was a straightforward trip, 'only three buses, and you're at Wimbledon. I'll meet you in the Wimpy Bar at Kingston, it's a lovely day, and you can go shopping.' She fell for it, and I was saved.

I walked around while waiting, frustrated at all these trolleys going unphotographed, and on the last day too. I finally met Mum and took possession of my other camera. She said she

Above:
'L3' No 1426 edges through the Kingston traffic on its way to the Richmond Park loop in the early afternoon sun. *Mick Webber*

Opposite above:
'L3s' Nos 1480 and 1431 in Kingston. No 1480 is about to turn right towards Tolworth and No 1431 heads for Wimbledon on the 604. *Mick Webber*

Opposite below:
'L3' No 1491 was new in wartime June 1940, and served the east of London well throughout. It was perhaps good that it should be allowed to finish its 22 years of service in the leafy suburbs of southwest London. *Mick Webber*

had arranged for us to get a cab back home that night, with a local friend who ran his own garage. How late could I persuade her to stay? Anyway, on to a 601 to Fulwell depot. The atmosphere there was, dare I say it, electric! Both ends of the depot were besieged with people milling around, and on the front yard No 1521 proudly stood, its booms decorated with bunting and balloons, highly polished for the occasion. These vehicles were too good to be just scrapped — I couldn't understand it — but scrapped they were, all except this creature here in front of me.

Throughout the day, a film crew with a camera perched on a van would follow vehicles about, recording the occasion. I recall some days earlier being invited to sit inside the lower deck of No 1477 in Fulwell depot, along with several other enthusiasts, and making believe we were travelling along, while they filmed us pretending to bounce and sway from side to side. It was here, inside a delicensed trolleybus, I decided to have a look at my stricken camera. Crouching under the stairs, I decided to wind off the remaining film and have a look inside. This I did and after prodding, poking, tapping and banging it, to my absolute delight, the shutter freed itself. This was particularly important, because this was the only camera for which I had a flash gun.

A late night stay was now definitely on the cards. I roamed around the yard noting other delicensed trolleys and, sitting on one to have a snack, I noticed that the door of my camera back was loose! 'How long had it been like this?', I thought. 'Has the light got in and ruined the film?' I managed to effect a repair by banging in the pin which held it in place but I was to discover later that the whole film had been spoiled.

I trudged through the rear yard out onto the road, to get a 601 for the ride to Tolworth, a chance to relax and take it all in. The vehicle was lightly loaded, and I well remember the pleasure I got from that journey, savouring every set of points, every acceleration from each stop, and the rumbling of the booms vibrating on the roof. The section by the Tolworth bypass wasn't disappointing either,

the driver happy to apply the power with a heavy foot. The journey back to Kingston through leafy Surbiton was a pleasant one, the sun now quite low, and my stomach told me that some sustenance was required. I met Mum in the trusty Wimpy Bar for food and to put into action my plan to persuade her that it was a good idea to stay to the end. After much debating, she agreed. I think she was actually enjoying it.

At this point we got a 604 to Hampton Court and as the darkness began to fall, made our way across the road to the 667 stop. We chatted to the conductor for a while, and he told us that the last one was due to be a 604, and that No 1521 would leave the depot later, although he didn't know when. We travelled up to Fulwell and I decided that some flash shots would be a good idea, so at the rear of the depot I took a 601 bound for Twickenham. We spent some time in the yard, wandering and just wondering what the place would be like without electric traction for the first time. I couldn't imagine it. The new Routemasters had been arriving all day, but I couldn't bring myself to show any interest in them.

Now was the time to find out what was going to happen with No 1521, as it was getting quite late. I spoke to an inspector about it and he told me that nobody would be allowed to board at the depot, but would have to wait at the usual pick-up point at Hampton Court. He told me what time it was due to leave, and advised us to get down there soon, in case there was a queue. So out we went to get a 667 back to Hampton Court.

Again, we spoke to the conductor of our plans, and he said that he didn't think we had a chance of getting on it. 'It'll be full before it gets to you', he said. I prayed that he would be wrong. Incidentally, he declined to take our fares: 'This is my last duty on a trolleybus; have this one on me.' When we got to the terminus, I jumped off and ran on ahead to the 604 boarding point. I couldn't believe it; there were only a couple of people there, no mighty queue as I had suspected. Leaving good old Mum to keep the place in the queue, I crossed the road to record No 1496 before she left on the 604 to travel in front of us, and then some 10min later, there she was: No 1521 appeared through the night and, to my utter delight, with plenty of room. The time, I think, was about 11.45pm.

Some people came running across the green to join us, as No 1521's booms were lowered to allow No 1496 to pass. Time here for a flash shot before we set off, then on board, where we sat downstairs nearside in the

Above right:
The sun is beginning to sink and the shadows lengthen as No 1526 arrives at Fulwell depot *en route* to Hampton Court. Interest is already beginning to show, as young boys with notebooks start to appear, as well as slightly older boys with cameras. *Mick Webber*

Right:
It is about 10.30pm and No 1497 pauses at the Stanley Road gate of Fulwell to drop off more people with cameras, before making one of its final journeys. *Mick Webber*

Opposite:
Elsewhere, Isleworth was seeing off its last trolleybus in style. No 1274 was painstakingly decorated inside and out and is caught here by the official photographer for *London Transport Magazine*. *London Transport*

middle. All of the bulbs were painted different colours.

As we set off, the trolleybus was still not full, but I noticed a small procession of cars following as we sped along Hampton Court Road. When we got to Kingston, a police car joined the queue, ringing its bells (yes, bells) and some singing broke out in the saloon. People were appearing along the route, standing in their night clothes at their front gates, waving goodbye, and when we reached Malden, the roundabout was full of people waving and cheering. To add to the occasion, at Raynes Park a publican emerged from his public house ringing a large handbell.

By the time we reached Wimbledon, the procession behind us stretched as far as I could see, and several hundred people were there to greet us. Not many managed to get on, however, as there were well over 100 already on board. The conductor came round for the fares for the return trip, and what a pity that no special tickets were made available; just the plain Gibson paper roll, without even the route number on it. Souvenir hunters immediately began removing items from the vehicle but were politely asked to replace them, 'until we get back to the depot'. The same publican was at Raynes Park on the return trip, and even more had gathered at Malden, including, I remember, a lady in a wheelchair, who waved her goodbye. Many more came to their gates to pay their respects along the way and the procession behind continued to grow.

When we left Kingston, the trip along Hampton Court Road was predictably enjoyable, always one of my favourite journeys. The following cars were now sounding their horns, and anyone who didn't know what was going on that night, was certainly now aware that something was happening. Hampton Court was reached and the points set for the depot at around 12.45am, and about half a mile before Fulwell, we were met by bus men and women with fog flares, who were there to lead us back home at a walking pace. This was when everything started to disappear. I still have the blue-painted bulb that was above my seat but where the rest went, I'll never know. It was here

that we got off, as I was anxious to get some photographs of this unforgettable night.

There were hundreds of people at the depot to greet No 1521 home, bright arc lights lit the scene and flash bulbs popped all around. As she reached the depot gates, progress became slower, and a large selection of the crowd burst into spontaneous song with 'Goodnight trolleys', which brought a lump to my throat. The journey through the gates seemed to take for ever and I seem to remember looking at my watch at 1.25am, and thinking, 'that's it, no more, it's all finished.' I looked up at the wires, wondering when the power would be turned off, and how long would it be before they cut them down, or was it all a dream, and would they all be running again in the morning?

Our taxi driver had been told to 'meet us at the depot gates'. Some chance; there were hundreds there milling around, and how we spotted his bald head shining under the arc lights, I shall never know. The journey home was a complete blur; I don't remember any of it. I just remember thinking how glad I was to have been part of it, and cursing my luck for being born too late to have been able to enjoy more of it.

Of course, I didn't realise at the time that I would be lucky enough to ride once more on No 1521, some 30 years later, in splendid condition at the Carlton Colville Museum. What a privilege that was. Why they haven't made a comeback like the tram, I fail to understand.

Below:
This is where we all get off. Although not until we're thrown off. 'L3' No 1521 arrives at Fulwell in the early hours of 9 May 1962, and the story is over. Thankfully it lives on at Carlton Colville.
Mick Webber

One of the most important ingredients for operating a successful trolleybus system is a smooth running and efficient maintenance department with reliable and dedicated staff. This London Transport certainly had in abundance.

In 1933 the LPTB inherited some ageing Tramways Department ADC tower wagons, but it was quite clear, once the decision had been taken to adopt the trolleybus, that some serious thinking must be directed towards their replacements. Between June and August 1935, eight AEC Mercury 4-ton tower wagons were delivered, numbered 150-157, later renumbered 75Q-82Q. Also during that summer, seven Leyland LB5 and LB4 buses, which had served with various independent operators prior to the LPTB takeover, were converted to 6-ton tower wagons as a stopgap measure. They were numbered 212L-218L.

In January 1936 NS760 was converted into an overhead wire lubricator and numbered 41H. It was later destroyed in the war. In May and June more NSs were withdrawn and transformed into 4½-ton tower wagons, Nos 187-194, which were later to become 21H-28H. August of the same year saw another batch of AEC Mercury 4-ton tower wagons arrive. These were numbered 195-202, later

CHAPTER 8
SERVICE AND MAINTENANCE

Below:
NS853 was converted into tower wagon No 188 in June 1936, and later, in June 1940, a cab was added. A linesman is at work here during the war years, the vehicle lasting through hostilities until May 1948, being renumbered 22H. Quadrant Picture Library

Leyland Cubs delivered in 1936.

In September 1937 three AEC Monarch 5-ton pole carriers were purchased and numbered 97N-99N. A further wire lubricator came into stock in March 1938, when T320 was converted and renumbered 114W. These curious vehicles were stationed at Rye Lane permanent way depot and endeavoured to lubricate the system at least once every two weeks, with a special lubricant made at Chiswick. In July 1938 two more AEC Monarch tower wagons with bodies by Eagles of Saltisford were delivered and originally numbered E26 and E27, although they later became 100N and 101N.

As the fleet grew in the latter prewar years, more of the successful trolleybus 'ambulances' were ordered, and the Albion version again arrived in February and March of 1939. There

changed to 83Q-90Q, and were all in stock by October, followed in November by Nos 205-210, which were AEC Mercury 5-ton pole carriers, later to become 91Q-96Q.

Perhaps the most interesting deliveries of 1936 were the 4-ton Leyland Cub trolleybus rescue trucks. Seven were delivered and numbered 169 and 218-223, later renumbered 189C and 203C-208C. They were equipped with spare wheels, supposedly one AEC and one Leyland, which could easily be off-loaded by way of a runway sunk into the floor, and down the hinged tailboards to ground level. Equipment cupboards were fitted along each side of the body and could be accessed from either side. The portion immediately behind the driver's cab was designed as a miniature workshop, with a canopy over for shelter. Light was provided inside, along with a bench top and vice. They soon became a familiar sight on the system and were always ready and quickly on the scene to repair punctures and other minor roadside breakdowns.

The growing system now had some new and some converted equipment to service the needs of the rapidly expanding network and many depots now received their own vehicles. In 1937 more breakdown tenders were ordered, this time based on the Albion chassis. Eight were delivered, numbered AN18-21 and AN30-33, later to become 121A-124A and 133A-136A. They followed the same design as the

were four delivered, carrying the numbers AN54-AN57, which were later to be 360A-363A. More tower wagons came in that July, when four AEC 4-ton Matadors, again with Eagle bodies, were delivered and numbered 412P-415P, a strange change-around in suffix letters. Into the war and another wire lubricator came, in the shape of No 422W, which was T306.

The department acquitted itself well during the war: 24 crews of linesman, mate and driver-operated, with three shifts over 24hr periods. Hundreds of incidents were recorded, ranging from damage to feeders to complete sections of wiring being rendered unusable. The crews came in for much praise in a Government booklet published in 1942:

Top:
In March 1938 T320 was converted into an overhead wire lubricator and numbered 114W. It was fitted with dummy booms which were used to grease the overhead wires with a substance made at the Chiswick laboratory. It is seen here in the Old Kent Road, almost opposite the entrance to the now closed bus garage, code P. *Michael Rooum*

Above right:
No 189C waits in the background, as its crew change a wheel on 'N1' No 1558. The trolleybus had suffered a puncture while operating on route 666 in Askew Road on 9 December 1961. *Mick Webber*

'They ran their bays of wire, 40 yards to a bay, over the trees in people's gardens when the standards had gone; in other places, notably in the Commercial Road, they found a new route, planted 43 poles for half a mile — and poles go in 6ft beneath the pavement.'

(It goes on to say) 'The message comes in one Saturday night, that a bomb had dropped at Southgate, destroyed a bus and blown down 12 bays of overhead wire. The flying squads, which are always out and ready during the raids, came out with their travelling towers, and got to work at once. They worked all night to the tune of shrapnel coming down on the roofs, and by five in the morning, the first bus passed through as usual.'

After the war, more tower wagons came into service to replace the ageing ADC units inherited from the tramways departments. These new additions came between February 1948 and October 1949 and were all converted from former STL class AEC Regent buses. They were allocated fleet numbers 722J-733J. In October 1948 STL12 was transformed into

Top:
414P was an AEC Matador 4-ton tower wagon dating from 1939, with bodywork by Eagles of Saltisford. It was originally in green livery, but was later painted red. It is seen here at work in North Finchley. *Michael Rooum*

Above:
A Leyland Cub attends to trolley boom problems encountered by 'C2' No 231 on route 645.

Above:
Most dewirements were minor run of the mill affairs, quickly corrected by the crews, but others could look quite spectacular, as can be seen here. 'F1' No 747 had been travelling towards Uxbridge when, at the junction with the 655 wires at Boston Road, it all went wrong. Trolley No 736 has come to a stop while the crew of the other vehicle move the booms out of the way. *Brian Speller*

Opposite:
Overhauls were shared between Fulwell and Charlton works, and this rare view at the latter shows just how interesting these places could be. Service vehicles, buses, a tram and a trolleybus, all in one picture, is not something easily achieved. *R. Hubble*

AIR LEAKAGE TESTS

Elmale ...DEPOT........ 5. 9. 1960

TROLLEYBUS NUMBERS		16 15	16 15 5-1-61	16 15 1.5-61
Time to compress from zero to cut out pressure	m. sec.	1·39	m. sec. 1-23	m. sec. 1·26
Time to compress from cutting in to cutting out	sec.	24	sec. 24	sec. 25
Governor pressure	cut in	lb. 64	lb. 64	lb. 65
	cut out	85	85	86
Drop in air pressure from max. in 2½ minutes	brake off	1½	1½	1½
	brake ON off	5	2½	3
Air alarm cut out pressure (signal arm rises)		45	46	46
Air alarm cut in pressure (signal arm falls)		58	56	58
Brake cylinder gauge reading at full brake application		65	66	66
Safety valve blow off pressure		108	108	105

REMARKS (state defects found and action taken figures to be forwarded) Retest

310/18
(10m, 7-52—C16—Stock) SIGNED

wire lubricator 734J, but this class of vehicle was to be relatively short-lived after the war; with the introduction of the long-insert carbon, they soon fell into disuse.

In March 1955 yet another STL was used, when No 2679 was converted into trolleybus towing lorry No 1009J. The last additions to the service fleet came in 1958, when in the first three months, five AEC Mercury 7-ton tower wagons and four pole carriers numbered 1073Q-1081Q were delivered. These were acquired solely for the purpose of dismantling the system and brought with them a cold wind of change.

Although some depots had their own tower wagons, in some cases housed in their own sheds, there were sheds located around the system to help cut down the time taken to attend to serious incidents, such as Garratt Lane, Earlsfield, Manor House and Islington.

All trolleybuses carried their own tool kit, which consisted of one saw, one fire extinguisher, one pair of rubber gloves, two spanners, one feeder pillar key, one telephone box kit and one budget lock key. Any driver opening his tool box was required to report the matter on his defect sheet. Specific instructions were given to crews, 'in the event of an accident rendering it necessary to raise the trolleybus'. They were to telephone the control office, who would decide either to send a breakdown tender, or that the crew should collect the lifting gear from the nearest emergency station ('as published from time to time in the traffic circular'). This would be done by driver or conductor, by the quickest means possible ('by taxicab if necessary'). The rule book then goes on to describe the means of lifting the vehicle, either at the side or at the front, and illustrates the method, which an inspector appears to execute with ease.

Depot staff were required to carry out daily leakage tests on all vehicles, and

forms were required to be filled out accordingly. Drivers were advised to check their brake pressure gauges at stops and were instructed to park their vehicle and ask for assistance should the reading drop below 50psi or exceed 120psi. Likewise, if the vacuum gauge fell below 12in, the vehicle must be parked. More paperwork would ensue for the driver should he find it necessary to use battery power, although some might just forget to note it down by the time they returned to the depot!

This means of movement was often very useful, and several official turns were authorised using this method; the South African vehicles undoubtedly suffered by not having this facility. To operate by battery propulsion, the driver would first make sure the circuit breakers were in the off position and also the reverser. He would then operate the battery/trolley changeover switch and place the reverser in the forward or reverse position. Lighting could be provided if required by moving the lighting switch to emergency.

Overhauls were carried out by Charlton and Fulwell works, on a ratio of about two to one in Fulwell's favour in the pre-1952 days, but once the trams had disappeared in that July, Charlton stepped up a gear and the balance was about equal. Some overhauls were dealt with at Chiswick tram depot in the prewar years, but this arrangement did not last. West

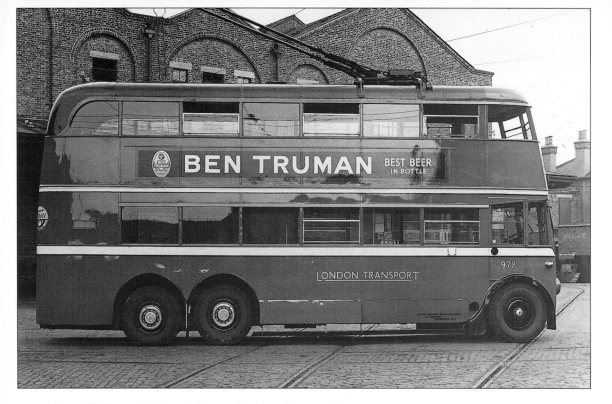

Above:
The standard of overhaul was always high at both establishments. 'J2' No 978 is seen here at Charlton works on 23 August 1946, showing off its broadside painted advertisement. *London Transport*

Ham Works carried out light overhauls and repaints, along with Fulwell, and these were turned out at about the rate of five a week from each establishment. Some depots had their electrical problems dealt with by Stonebridge, and due to the poor facilities at Wandsworth, all but the very minor problems found there were rectified by Hammersmith. After each minor or major overhaul, the vehicle concerned would receive a date and the letter 'P' or 'C' on its inside rear platform wall; the 'P' to denote partial and the 'C' to show complete overhaul.

In later years the depots were evenly split on where their vehicles were taken. Bexleyheath, Bow, Clapton, Finchley, Ilford, Lea Bridge, Poplar, Stamford Hill, Walthamstow and West Ham sent theirs to Charlton, with Fulwell taking the others. Overhaul of all major electrical components were carried out at Charlton's engineering shops. Charlton finished its overhauling days in 1959, when 'N2' No 1669 became the last vehicle to be treated, and Fulwell followed in 1961, when 'Q1' No 1768 emerged, a vehicle that now resides in the LT collection, as does tower wagon No 89Q.

As a result of the Tram & Trolleybus Department merger with Central Buses in July 1950, many economies were made but, fortunately for the trolleybus fleet, changes to its livery were not among them. The bus fleet was subjected to a number of changes throughout the 1950s, all of them resulting in a more lacklustre and drab appearance.

The trolleybus fleet was finished in standard London Transport red and carried a cream band below the lower deck windows and another between decks at upper floor level. Both of these bands were lined out in black and black beading was applied below the upper deck windows. Mudguards were also black, apart from the rear ones on vehicles with metal mudguards, these being red. Vehicles were delivered with silver roofs, although during 1938 they began to appear with red front domes, and after war was declared, the silver gave way to a shade of matt brown. The rear dome was changed to brown gloss after the war.

The distinctive trolleybus emblem was applied to the front centre of the vehicle below the driver's screens, on the lower nearside between the rear mudguard and the platform, and on the rear lower panel. The rear position was later changed during the war to the rear platform window, and the nearside emblem was omitted from 1953 onwards.

Inside, the vehicles had white ceilings on both decks, but differed in other respects. Nos 95A, 107A, 612A, 803A and 1565A all had 'Alhambrinal' cream-covered lower deck ceilings. The lower saloon was predominantly

CHAPTER 9
ODDS AND ENDS

Below:
Posed for the camera on 20 June 1949, 'F1' No 698 perfectly displays the London trolleybus livery. Distinctive features are the black lining out of the cream bands and black beading under the upper deck windows, together with the distinctive trolleybus emblem on the front panel and on the side near to the platform, although the latter was to disappear.
London Transport

green and brown, while the upper was finished in two-tone blue, although green and brown was standard on both decks after the war, with a few exceptions. The South African vehicles had polished wood window surrounds and panelling covered in brown Rexine. Nos 64-182 originally had red rear mudguards, which were quite deep and covered some of the tyre. This also applied to many of the other vehicles built up to about October 1938, which were delivered with black rubber wings, also partially covering the tyre. These were all cut back to a shallower style shortly afterwards. AEC vehicles retained their chrome-plated wheel fittings to the end, while the Leyland fleet had polished aluminium wheel rings.

Seats were aluminium-framed and the moquette was basically a brown and blue floral pattern on the lower deck, and shades of blue on the upper. After the war the style changed to the green and brown pattern that was so familiar in the 1950s, or the bus-style moquette which it shared with the RT family buses.

Overall length was 27ft 6in in the case of the short-wheelbase 60-seaters, and 30ft for the long-wheelbase 70-seaters. Height unladen, to the top of the trolley booms, was 15ft 7in and the booms themselves were 19ft 6in from

Opposite above:
'D1' No 384, as shown by Leyland's photographer early in 1936. This shows the half-width bulkhead layout with driver-facing seat, as was standard on the first trolleybuses. It was converted to full-width bulkhead in 1938.
©*The British Commercial Vehicle Museum Trust Archives*

Opposite below:
Another interior, this time the upper deck of Park Royal bodied 'E3' No 641. Delivered in May 1937, it was destroyed by enemy action at West Ham works on 30 July 1944.
©*The British Commercial Vehicle Museum Trust Archives*

Below:
Posed on 27 May 1948 is 'K1' No 1133, to show potential advertisers what impression could be gained by using the offside of a trolleybus to highlight their products. Many advertisements were signwritten directly on to the vehicles during this period. *London Transport*

gantry to the shoe. The width, apart from the 'Q1' and 'SA' classes, was 7ft 6in.

The seats downstairs were spaced at 2ft 6in intervals from the handrail on one seat to the handrail on the next, but in the upper saloon the spaces were 2ft 4$\frac{1}{2}$in on the nearside and 2ft 4in on the offside. This gradually staggered the seats, leaving a space for freedom of movement at the top of the stairs. Apart from handrails, three floor to ceiling stanchions were provided in the upper deck aisle and two

in the lower deck. All seats were 2ft 10$\frac{1}{4}$in wide, giving an aisle width of 1ft 3in in the lower saloon and 1ft 1in in the upper. They were designed to have an unladen platform height of 1ft 5in maximum from the ground level, reducing to 1ft 2in when laden. Ceiling heights were 5ft 10$\frac{1}{2}$in downstairs and 5ft 8$\frac{1}{2}$in upstairs. These dimensions were laid down by London Transport in their general arrangement drawing.

Electrical equipment was mainly installed in the cab, indeed No 553 and Nos 1055 onwards were all built in this way, the rest of the fleet having the equipment chassis-mounted.

Each vehicle was fitted with 'coin testers', to check for foreign or forged coins. These were fixed just below the last offside upper deck window at the top of the stairs and alongside the fare chart in the lower saloon. They were metal fitments with slots cut into them, each one corresponding with the thickness of coins of the day. As on the bus fleet, two convex mirrors were fitted to aid the conductor, one

half-way up the stairs, and one at the top fixed to the ceiling. The upper deck ceilings were fitted with two circular, chrome-plated ventilator grilles.

Destination blinds were changed by the conductor from the stairs in the case of the rear but the front blinds were changed by the driver in the case of Nos 755, 780-904 and 920 onwards, the rest being operated by the conductor from the upper deck. The side blinds were also operated by the conductor from the upper deck, except in the case of the 'Q1s', which were changed by a handle from the platform. Until the merger with Central Buses, trolleybuses carried just an enamelled running number plate, fitted each side just behind the cab at waist level. After the merger, however, they adopted the garage code aluminium stencil plates as used by the bus fleet. From about 1960, these codes were painted on the vehicle in white.

Although dealt with excellently elsewhere in other books, it is worth mentioning briefly the power supply. Current to the running wire was supplied at 600V dc, fed by 102 substations scattered around the system and relayed by feeder boxes. A new design of box was supplied by Bradshaw and Son of Retford, displaying the LT bull's-eye styling. The tubular steel support poles which carried the cables from these boxes were painted with a white band, to remind drivers that they should not draw power as the vehicle passed under these sections.

The legal requirement was for the negative wire to be on the nearside and the positive wire on the offside of the road. Principal suppliers of power were London Transport's own power stations at Greenwich, Neasden and Chelsea, although various electricity companies and local authorities also participated. Generally speaking, the steel

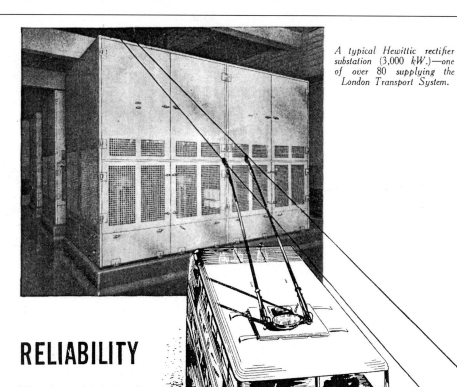

A typical Hewittic rectifier substation (3,000 kW.)—one of over 80 supplying the London Transport System.

RELIABILITY

The dependability of the trolleybus service is taken for granted. But the trolleybus is not only dependable, it is *dependent*—upon the reliability of the converting plant that provides its D.C. supply. More often than not this will comprise the most dependable of all modern converting plant:—

OVER A MILLION kW. IN SERVICE

HACKBRIDGE AND HEWITTIC ELECTRIC CO. LTD., WALTON-ON-THAMES, SURREY

Telephone: Walton-on-Thames 760 (8 lines)   Telegrams: " Electric," Walton-on-Thames

support poles were available in four different qualities and four different lengths; at certain places the overhead employed wall stays and brackets.

As an addition to a Traffic Circular issued in February 1950, the Tram & Trolleybus Department supplied a list of 'Authorised Refreshment Places'. All the remaining tram and most trolleybus routes were listed, together with names and addresses of cafés and other establishments where the crews might seek refreshment. Crews on route 543/643 were advised to get their tea at the City Coach Co Canteen at Wood Green, while 627 crews could call at the LT hut at Edmonton Town Hall. There were also canteen huts at Craven Park, Waltham Cross and Hampton Court, although 654 drivers and conductors were advised of Betty's Café in Anerley Road and crews on the 557, 697 and 699 were directed to Sid's Café in Chingford

Road. Route 602 crews were told to use Mrs Rawlin's General Store at the Dittons and asked to order refreshments on northbound journeys and collect on the southbound trip.

Trolleybuses, like the trams, were renowned for moving large crowds quickly and efficiently, especially at big sporting events. The *London Transport Magazine* of November 1948 dealt with the subject. It chose a week in that September and relates the crowds that were moved during the seven-day period by the Northern Section.

Above:
'K2' No 1200 from Wood Green on training duties on 1 February 1961. Drivers were trained on trolleybuses right up to the last months before replacement.

Monday:	Football — Tottenham 33,700; West Ham 18,000
Tuesday:	Speedway — West Ham 45,000
Wednesday:	Greyhounds — Clapton 5,500; Harringay 7,500; Hendon 4,300; Walthamstow 6,500; Wembley 7,250; West Ham 5,800
Thursday:	Football — Leyton 12,000; Speedway — Wembley 85,000
Friday:	Speedway — Harringay 24,000
Saturday:	Football — Tottenham 60,500; West Ham 22,000; and five other matches totalling 40,000; Greyhound meetings as Wednesday — 67,000

Quite a formidable task, and an eye-opener into the venues and events that were around before television took over completely. The article gives a fascinating account of preparations for extras for the Wembley Cup Final. It was estimated that match crowds could be catered for with the normal service (662) plus 22 extras, while the requirement for post-match extras would be 40. All this bearing in mind that the Underground took a large number of the fans home. The description of the build-up for this event is as follows:

'H hour, in operation Cup Final, is usually around Friday midnight, when the extras, driven by men of the Rolling Stock Department, and helped out by traffic drivers, roll out of the depots throughout the Northern Division on their journey through the silent streets to Stonebridge Depot. Further reinforcements converge on Stonebridge at the end of am peak. Working to a supplementary schedule of journeys between Paddington and Wembley, and Scrubs Lane and Wembley, on route 662, the volunteer crews, working overtime on their rest days, take the extras out to deal with the spread-over forward traffic. As this work is completed, the extras are lined up at Stonebridge. As the time of the "break" moment, when a vast crowd starts to pour out of the ground, draws near, the trolleybuses are dispatched, at 2min

intervals, to Sudbury terminus. There they turn round, and run back to Wembley High Road. The first four run on to the layby wire, installed at Wembley Hill Road loading point, to enable service buses to run through. The other extras line up in Wembley Hill Road with poles down.

'The game is over. The spectators swarm out, the first two buses are full. A bang on the side from the inspectors in charge of loading, and they are away. The next two move up to load. Their place is taken by two signalled down by the district superintendent. They coast downhill into the layby with poles down. While they await their move to the stop, up go the poles. It is their turn now. On a few yards, load, the bell and off they go. Tests proved that it takes 1min 30sec to fill a trolleybus. That is the time allowed. Twenty seconds to move up to the stop in the layby. Ten seconds to spare. The loading of 60 buses an hour is easily held. This year there was no queue, as the crowds arrived they were loaded.'

The magazine then goes on to point out that at Tottenham the task is even greater, as there is no nearby Underground station to help with the job. A total of 46 extras, with crews from Edmonton, Stamford Hill, Highgate, Wood Green and Walthamstow, were used:

'Trolleybuses cannot be conveniently lined up for the return traffic but must be scheduled to arrive minute by minute, at the layby wire. Queue control is difficult, as the crowd is disgorged directly on the two loading points. But in spite of these drawbacks, the cup-tie crowd of 69,000 last February was cleared in a record time of 53min from the final whistle.'

Fulham FC and the Boat Race also get mentioned, and the turning point at Bishops Park (Edgarley Terrace) is said to have proved a great help in running these extras. Mitcham Fair was another event covered; when it resumed in August 1948 after an absence of 10 years, 30 extras were run from Sutton, Wandsworth and Hammersmith.

A part from the roles of Acton and Chiswick in the early prewar years, London trolleybuses operated out of 21 depots. We now deal with these in alphabetical order, starting with Bexley, which was the only new depot built on a site not formerly occupied by tramway property. It was built in Erith Road and opened on 10 November 1935, had a capacity of 75, and was converted to buses on 3 March 1959. It was coded BX in 1950 and No 412B performed the last rites.

Bow depot was situated in Fairfield Road. It was equipped with a turntable traverser and had space for 102 vehicles. It was given the code BW in 1950 and was converted to buses on 18 August 1959. Run-ins showed 'BOW CHURCH' on their blinds. The last trolleybus home was No 1610. It was built by the LCC and opened in 1908.

Edmonton was inherited from the Metropolitan Electric Tramways, having been opened in 1880 by the North London Suburban Tramways and becoming MET-owned in 1902. It was extensively rebuilt and had two turntable traversers and space for 122 vehicles. It was coded EM. It was situated at the end of Tramway Avenue and was converted on 18 July 1961 after No 1238 had

CHAPTER 10
DEPOTS

Below:
The only completely new depot not on former tramway land was at Bexleyheath. No 115 waits at the rear of the depot while No 95, whose body was to be destroyed in the war, and others shelter inside. The date is November 1935, and the wiring is very nearly complete. *London Transport*

2 January 1962, after No 1468 had arrived home. It was eventually closed on 4 December 1993.

Fulwell depot, the home of London Trolleybuses, was opened in 1902 by the London United Tramways. It was built between Stanley and Wellington Roads, having an entrance in both, with cover for 120 vehicles. A substantial works building also occupied part of the site but has since been sold. It was given the code FW and was the last depot to operate trolleybuses in London, No 1521 being the very last one home in the early hours of 9 May 1962, after 11,316 days of trolleybus operation.

Hackney, later renamed Clapton, and coded CT in 1950, was opened by the LCC in 1909. Located in Bohemia Place, it had space for 90 trolleybuses and was provided with a turntable traverser. It lost its trolleybuses on 14 April 1959, after No 1243 came in. The run-ins showed 'HACKNEY STATION'.

Hammersmith depot in Great Church Street was opened by the LCC in 1908, and was completely rebuilt for trolleybuses and equipped with a turntable traverser. Coded HB in 1950, it housed 65 vehicles and was closed after conversion on 19 July 1960, No 1161

arrived. It was closed on 31 January 1986, and has since been demolished.

Finchley depot was built by the MET and opened in 1905. It was situated in Woodberry Road, had a turntable traverser and accommodated 108 vehicles. It was coded FY in 1950 and was converted to buses on

being the final run-in. After a spell as the home of the BEA coaches, it was finally demolished.

Hanwell, in the Broadway, was opened in 1908 by the London United Tramways, and was rebuilt for trolleybuses and given a turntable traverser. Its capacity was 108 and the code HL was allotted in 1950. Last day was 8 November 1960, and No 1812 was the last one home, showing 'HANWELL BROADWAY'. The building was closed on 27 March 1993 and demolished in 1996.

Hendon, renamed Colindale, and coded CE in 1950, was a former MET shed built in 1904 with substantial overhaul facilities at the rear. It was situated on the east side of Edgware Road and housed 48 vehicles. Conversion came on 2 January 1962, and with it came closure and later demolition. No 1564 was the last one home.

Holloway depot, later coded HT and renamed Highgate, was opened by the LCC in 1907. It had three traversers and was situated in Pemberton Gardens. It was converted on 25 April 1961, No 1554 being the last home. Capacity was 230.

Hounslow, later changed to Isleworth and given the code IH, was a complete rebuild of the former London United shed in London Road, originally built in 1901. It was equipped with a turntable traverser and had a capacity of

Top:
The new and the old in Hanwell depot on 6 November 1960. There are two days to go before trolleybus abandonment and trainer RM142 stands alongside 'Q1' No 1813, in a strangely empty depot. Who could have guessed that the trolleybus would soon be on its way to Spain! *Brian Speller*

Above:
'SA3' No 1756 sits half in Ilford depot in 1959. It is clear by the filled-in brick arches above the doors how the depot used to look in tramway days. It looks as though the photographer has caught the milkman delivering. *Brian Speller*

37. No 1274 was the last in in the early hours of 9 May 1962 and the depot never opened its doors to public transport again.

Ilford depot was situated in Ley Street and was opened by Ilford Corporation in 1903. It received the code ID in 1950 and had a capacity of 34 vehicles. It was closed after the conversion on 18 August 1959, No 1756 being the last one in.

Above:
Nos 71 and 72 stand alongside each other in the newly converted Sutton depot on 7 February 1936. The wiring contractor Clough Smith has yet to collect its horse-drawn tower wagons. *London Transport*

Opposite above:
An excellent view of the pits at Wood Green. 'H1s' Nos 830, 776, 818 and 759 are among those being worked on in January 1947. *London Transport*

Opposite below:
A wartime picture taken on 18 October 1940 shows some clearing up after minor bomb damage. 'D3' No 552 sports its wartime white markings and headlamp masks, although window netting had not yet been applied. *London Transport*

Leyton depot was opened in 1889 by Leyton Corporation and taken over by the LCC in 1921. Occupying a site in Lea Bridge Road, it was renamed Lea Bridge in 1950 and coded LB. It was closed after conversion on 14 April 1959, the last one in being No 1327. Capacity was 33.

Poplar depot was in Leven Road and was opened by the LCC in 1906. It had a turntable traverser and was coded PR in 1950. Conversion took place on 10 November 1959 and No 1464 was the last one in. Capacity was 149 and the building was subsequently closed on 2 November 1985.

Stamford Hill depot in Rookwood Road was opened by the LCC in 1907. It had two traversers and space for 97 vehicles. It was coded SF in 1950 and was converted on 18 July 1961, No 1326 being the last one in.

Stonebridge Park was inherited from the MET, who opened the premises in Harrow Road in 1906. It was given the code SE in 1950 and converted to buses after traffic on 2 January 1962, No 1666 closing operations. The capacity was 86 and it was finally closed down on 15 August 1981.

Sutton depot, renamed Carshalton and coded CN in 1950, was in Westmead Road, and was built by the South Metropolitan Tramways, opening in 1906. It was completely rebuilt and equipped with a turntable traverser, and had a capacity of 51. Last day of operation was 3 March 1959 and the last one in before the buses took over was No 83. It was finally closed to traffic on 28 January 1964.

Walthamstow depot was opened by Walthamstow Corporation in Chingford Road in 1905. It had a turntable traverser and room for 107 trolleybuses. Conversion came on 26 April 1960 and No 685 was the final bus home. It was coded WW and was finally closed on 23 November 1991. It has since been demolished.

Wandsworth depot in Jew's Row was acquired from the LCC and originated in 1883. It was converted, along with its trams, on 30 September 1950, and therefore never received a code as a trolleybus depot (becoming WD in bus days). It had capacity for 24 trolleybuses to operate alongside its trams and had a turntable traverser. It was eventually closed on 10 July 1987.

West Ham was opened by the Corporation in 1906, built on land in Greengate Street. It also had a works building alongside. The code WH was applied in 1950 and conversion came on 26 April 1960, No 622 being the last one home, having been also the first to operate from here when new. It was closed on 9 October 1992 and has since been demolished.

Wood Green depot, in the High Road, was a former MET shed built originally in 1895. It was partially rebuilt for trolleybuses and equipped with a turntable traverser, having space for 108 vehicles. It was coded WN and was converted on 7 November 1961. No 1353 was the last one in.

Depots, generally speaking, operated either AEC or Leyland vehicles. Those regarded to be AEC sheds were Bow, Colindale, Fulwell, Finchley, Isleworth, Poplar, Stonebridge, Highgate and West Ham, and the Leyland counterparts were Bexleyheath, Carshalton, Hanwell, Hammersmith, Edmonton, Clapton, Lea Bridge, Stamford Hill, Wood Green and Wandsworth. Ilford, and to a degree Walthamstow, operated a mix of the two. Fulwell, Isleworth and Hanwell later operated BUTs.

The scrapping, or dismantling as it was then referred to, of London's huge trolleybus system was a lucrative business. One company in particular was synonymous with the task, and that was George Cohen & Son of the 600 Group. They had finished off the South London tram fleet in 1952 and had received some contracts earlier to scrap LUT Diddlers at Poplar depot. They paid LT just over £100 per vehicle and overhead was said to fetch around £240 per ton. In all, over 10,000 tons of metal was salvaged. Glass was not saved, however, it being too uneconomic to release the 50 or more screws that held each pane in place.

Cohens had three locations at which they performed these tasks; their own yard at Bidder Street in Canning Town, London Transport's own property at Penhall Road in Charlton and the land to the rear of Colindale

depot. Thirty-four were dealt with at Canning Town, 87 at Charlton, and the rest at Colindale. Scrapping at Charlton had ceased by September 1959.

A few other contractors did, however, get their hands on some trolleybuses. Birds of Stratford-upon-Avon received 160 to deal with; Thompsons of Cardiff were given 50; Cox & Danks yard at Devons Road, Bow, took 22, and one each went to W. North of Leeds (No 494)

CHAPTER 11
SCRAPPING

Below:
Not much comment needed here. The workman cuts up a steering column, while No 442, standing on the edge of the tram traverser pit, awaits its turn for the cutter's torch. The scene is Penhall Road, Charlton.
Ron Harrington

and Lunger of London (No 304). One wonders at the economies of towing a vehicle to Cardiff or Stratford-upon-Avon!

To return to Cohens, their staff magazine for the summer of 1960 stated that they would be removing 24,000 traction poles from the street, with some 200 miles of overhead, but by the time the summer 1962 edition appeared, they had amended their figures to read 28,000 poles and 240 miles of overhead. Several councils did purchase the traction poles *in situ*, for use as lamp standards, West Ham being the largest customer, and indeed some can still be seen in the east of London and Docklands. Cohens proudly presented No 1521 to the Historical Commercial Vehicle Club after withdrawal in May 1962. Thought to have escaped the cutter's torch were Nos 1637, 1641, 1653/5/6/7/8/9, which were put into store at Fulwell Works after withdrawal at stage 13 in January 1962. Rumours were rife that they had been sold for further service overseas, and indeed something must have been in the air for LT to have moved them south, but whatever it may have been, it did not come to fruition and they eventually ended up at Colindale and became the last to be scrapped, No 1653 being the final one in September 1962.

Ironically, Cohens supplied and advised Park Royal on lifting and mechanical equipment used in the Routemaster construction programme, and their sister company, G. Beaton & Sons, supplied the tubular seat frames, cab screens and windows for the new buses.

Below:
Apart from scrapping the trolleybuses, Cohens dismantled much of the overhead and traction poles. A bracket arm pole has just been uprooted, and the all-conquering Routemaster passes by. The scene is Canning Town, Trinity Church. *Ron Harrington*

Opposite:
Penhall Road again, and No 799B has had its upper deck unceremoniously removed, its last service days at Bexleyheath now but a memory. *Ron Harrington*

Above:
Colindale on 24 March 1962, and 'K' class Leyland booms sway desperately in the breeze. *Mick Webber*

Right:
The unwanted distinction of being the very last London trolleybus to be scrapped goes to 'N2' No 1653. It was one of eight sent to Fulwell amid rumours of a sale for further service but this did not materialise and they were sent to Colindale for scrapping. This view was taken on 22 August 1962, and the vehicle was scrapped the following month. *Mick Webber*

TABLE 1 FLEET LIST

Fleet Nos	Reg No Series	Class	AEC	Leyland	Above Screen	Side Mounted	Below Screen	Unit Construction	Chassisless Construction	Body	Motor	Controller	Class Delivered During	Radiused Front Upper Windows
1-35	HX, MG	A1	35	–	–	✔	–	–	–	U.C.C.	E.E.	E.E.	2/31 – 7/31	–
36-60	MG, MV	A2	25	–	–	✔	–	–	–	U.C.C.	B.T.H.	B.T.H.	8/31 – 12/31	–
61	AHX 801	X1	1	–	–	✔	–	–	–	L.G.O.C.[1]	E.E.	E.E.	3/33	Part
62	AXU 188	X2	1	–	✔	–	–	–	–	M.C.C.W.	M.V.	M.V.	7/34	–
63	AXU 189	X3	1	–	–	✔	–	–	–	E.E.	E.E.	E.E.	8/34	–
64-93	CGF	B1	–	30	✔	–	–	–	–	B.R.C.W.	M.V.	M.V.	11/35 – 1/36	–
94-131	CGF	B2	–	38	✔	–	–	–	–	BRUSH	M.V.	M.V.	10/35 – 12/35	–
132-141	CGF	C1	10	–	✔	–	–	–	–	WEYMANN	E.E.	E.E.	10/35 – 11/35	–
142-183	CGF	C1	42	–	✔	–	–	–	–	M.C.C.W.	E.E.	E.E.	10/35 – 11/35	–
184-283	CUL	C2	100	–	–	✔	–	–	–	M.C.C.W.	E.E.	E.E.	3/36 – 1/37	–
284-383	CUL	C3	100	–	–	✔	–	–	–	B.R.C.W.	E.E.	E.E.	3/36 – 1/37	–
384	CUL	D1	–	1	–	✔	–	–	–	LEYLAND	M.V.	M.V.	4/36	–
385-483	DGY	D2	–	99	–	✔	–	–	–	M.C.C.W.	M.V.	M.V.	10/36 – 5/37	–
484-488	DGY	B3	–	5	✔	–	–	–	–	B.R.C.W.	M.V.	M.V.	all 9/36	–
489-493	DGY	B1	–	5	✔	–	–	–	–	B.R.C.W.	M.V.	M.V.	all 9/36	–
494-553	DLY	D3	–	60	–	✔	–	–	–	B.R.C.W.	M.V.	M.V.	5/37 – 11/37	–
554-603	DLY	E1	50	–	–	✔	–	–	–	BRUSH	E.E.	M.V.	5/37 – 11/37	–
604-628	DLY	E2	25	–	–	✔	–	–	–	WEYMANN	E.E.	M.V.	4/37 – 6/37	–
629-653	DLY	E3	25	–	–	✔	–	–	–	PARK ROYAL	E.E.	M.V.	3/37 – 6/37	–
654-753	DLY	F1	–	100	–	✔	674	–	–	LEYLAND	M.V	M.V.	3/37 – 12/37	–
754	DLY	X4	1	–	–	✔	–	–	✔	L.P.T.B.[2]	M.V.	M.V.	4/37	–
755-904	ELB	H1	–	150	–	✔	–	–	–	M.C.C.W.	M.V.	M.V.	2/38 – 10/38	–
905-951	ELB	J1	47	–	–	✔	–	–	–	WEYMANN	M.V.	E.E.	2/38 – 4/38	–
952	ELB	J1	1	–	–	✔	–	–	–	M.C.C.W.	M.V.	E.E.	2/38	–
953	ELB	M1	1	–	–	✔	–	✔	–	WEYMANN	M.V.	E.E.	2/38	✔
954	ELB	L2	1	–	–	✔	–	–	✔	M.C.C.W.	M.V.	E.E.	3/38	–
955-1029	ELB, EXV[3]	J2	75	–	–	✔	–	–	–	B.R.C.W.	M.V.	E.E.	2/38 – 6/38	–
1030-1054	EXV	J3	25	–	–	✔	–	–	–	B.R.C.W.	M.V.	E.E.	8/38 – 10/38	–
1055-1154	EXV	K1	–	100	–	✔	–	–	–	LEYLAND	M.V.	M.V.	10/38 – 3/39	–
1155-1254	EXV	K2	–	100	–	✔	–	–	–	LEYLAND	M.V.	E.E.	10/38 – 3/39	–
1255-1304	EXV	K1	–	50	–	✔	–	–	–	LEYLAND	M.V.	M.V.	3/39 – 6/39	–
1305-1354	EXV	K2	–	50	–	✔	–	–	–	LEYLAND	M.V.	E.E.	3/39 – 6/39	–
1355-1369	EXV	L1	15	–	–	✔	–	–	✔	M.C.C.W.	M.V.	E.E.	3/39 – 6/39	✔
1370-1378	EXV	L2	9	–	–	✔	–	–	✔	M.C.C.W.	M.V.	E.E.	all 6/39	✔
1379	EXV	X5	1	–	–	–	✔	–	✔	M.C.C.W.	M.V.	E.E.	6/39	✔
1380-1529	FXF FXH	L3	150	–	–	–	✔	–	✔	M.C.C.W.	M.V.	M.V.	8/39 – 6/40	✔
1530-1554	FXH	M1	25	–	–	–	✔	✔	–	WEYMANN	M.V.	E.E	11/39 – 1/40	✔
1555-1644	FXH	N1	90	–	–	–	✔	–	–	B.R.C.W.	M.V.	E.E.	6/39 – 6/40	✔
1645-1669	FXH	N2	25	–	–	–	✔	–	–	PARK ROYAL	M.V.	E.E.	11/39 – 6/40	✔
1670	FXH	X6	1	–	–	–	✔	–	✔	E.E	M.V	E.E.	1/40	✔
1671	DTD 649	X7	–	1	–	✔	–	–	✔	LEYLAND	M.V.	M.V.	(2/39) 9/39	–
1672-1696	GGP	K3	–	25	–	–	✔	–	–	LEYLAND	M.V.	E.E.	10/40 – 12/40	–
1697-1721	GGP	P1	–	25	–	–	✔	–	–	M.C.C.W.	M.V.	E.E.	1/41 – 10/41	✔
1722-1733	GGW GLB	SA1	–	12	–	–	✔	–	–	M.C.C.W.	G.E.C.	G.E.C.	11/41 – 2/42	–
1734-1746	GLB	SA2	–	13	–	–	✔	–	–	M.C.C.W.	M.V.	M.V.	3/42 – 8/42	–
1747-1764	GLB	SA3	18	–	–	–	✔	–	–	M.C.C.W.	E.E.	E.E.	6/42 – 6/43	✔
1765-1841	HYM[4]	Q1	77[4]	–	–	–	✔	–	–	M.C.C.W.	M.V.	E.E.[5]	2/48 – 3/49	✔
1842-1891	LYH[4]	Q1	50[4]	–	–	–	✔	–	–	M.C.C.W.	M.V.	E.E.	5/52 – 12/52	✔
			1027 (Includes BUT)	864				26	179					

NOTES

1. Chiswick
2. Charlton
3. No 1000: EXX 10
4. BUT chassis: 127
5. Except No 1841 (MV)

Classes B1, J3, L1 & X5 fitted with coasting and runback brakes

Right:
Malden Road, Kentish Town, is the location for this view of 'M1' No 1551 on route 639. The 'M1s' were unit-constructed AECs with Weymann bodywork and dated from November 1939 to January 1940. *C. Carter*

TABLE 2 FLEET ANALYSIS BY BODYWORK MANUFACTURERS

FLEET NOS	REG NO. SERIES	CLASS	UCC	LGOC	MCCW	EE	BRCW	BRUSH	WEY-MANN	LEYLAND	PARK ROYAL	LPTB	WEYMANN 'A'	EAST LANCS 'B'	NCB 'C'	BEADLE REBUILD
1-35	HX MG	A1	35													
36-60	MG MV	A2	25													
61	AHX 801	X1		1												
62	AXU A88	X2			1											
63	AXU 189	X3				1										
64-93	CGF	B1					30									
94-131	CGF	B2						38					2		2	
132-141	CGF	C1								10						
142-183	CGF	C1			42											
184-283	CUL	C2			100											
284-383	CUL	C3					100									
384	CUL	D1									1					
385-483	DGY	D2			99								1	10	8	5¹
484-488	DGY	B3					5									
489-493	DGY	B1					5									
494-553	DGY	D3					60									
554-603	DLY	E1						50							3	
604-628	DLY	E2							25				1			
629-653	DLY	E3									25				2	
654-753	DLY	F1								100					5	
754	DLY	X4										1				
755-904	ELB	H1			150								4	9		2
905-951	ELB	J1							47							
952	ELB	J1			1											
953	ELB	M1							1							
954	ELB	L2			1											
955-1029	ELB EXV²	J2					75						1	3		
1030-1054	EXV	J3					25									
1055-1154	EXV	K1								100			2			1³
1155-1254	EXV	K2								100			2			
1255-1304	EXV	K1								50			1			
1305-1354	EXV	K2								50						
1355-1369	EXV	L1			15											
1370-1378	EXV	L2			9											
1379	EXV	X5			1											
1380*-1529	FXF*, FXH	L3			150										1	
1530-1554	FXH	M1							25						2	
1555-1644	FXH	N1					90						2			
1645-1669	FXH	N2									25					
1670	FXH	X6				1										
1671	DTD 649	X7								1						
1672-1696	GGP	K3								25						
1697-1721	GGP	P1			25											
1722-1733	GGW, GLB	SA1			12											
1734-1746	GLB	SA2			13											
1747-1764	GLB	SA3			18											
1765-1841	HYM	Q1			77											
1842-1891	LYH	Q1			50											
			60	1	764	2	390	88	108	427	50	1	16	25	20	8

NOTES

1   including No 406A
2   No 1000: EXX 10
3   No 1123A

Above right:
'N1' No 1561 negotiates the Jubilee Clock at Harlesden on route 662, on what appears to be a dreary, damp Saturday. The 'N1s' and 'N2s' were the last standard AEC trolleybuses to be received by London Transport. *Michael Rooum*

Right:
No 1035 was a 'J3', fitted with coasting and runback brakes for route 611. They had BRCW bodywork, and this vehicle, shown here at the Nags Head, lasted until April 1960. *C. Carter*

Opposite:
Awaiting delivery to its depot is 'K2' No 1315, looking splendid after its overhaul at Fulwell Works. How times change: note the side advertisement proclaiming that Test cricketer Frank Tyson smokes Capstan!

TABLE 3 SEQUENCE OF INCIDENTS CAUSING TROLLEYBUSES TO BE DESTROYED OR REBODIED

DATE	Depot to which Allocated when Damaged or Destroyed (some incidents were while on the road)	Damaged & rebodied By Weymann as 'A'	[1] 'B'	[2] 'C'	Destroyed
07.SEP.40	BW	1565A			
18.SEP.40	SF	1128A			
27.SEP.40	HT	107A			
11.OCT.40	CT	1244A			
11.OCT.40	WW	1285A			
13.OCT.40	WN	861A			
13.OCT.40	HT	1001A			
07.NOV.40	BX	95A, 406A, 792A, 795A			
08.NOV.40	SF	1123A			
09.MAR.41	WH	621A			
09.MAR.41	WH'	803A, 1247A			1492
19.MAR.41	BW	1587A			
11.NOV.42	HT'				1365
LATE.43	WH'				953
29.JUNE.44	BX		17 [3]	9 [4]	12 [5]
27.JULY.44	WW				1387
30.JULY.44	WH'		8 [6]	10 [7]	364
16.AUG.44	WW			575C	
Total: 18 events	1+1 1+1 1+1 1 1+1+1 1 4+38 1 3+19 1 1	16	25	20	17
	78(including 1001 twice)	61 (including 1001 twice)			
		78 (including 1001 twice)			

1] DAMAGED AND REBODIED BY EAST LANCS AS 'B'

2] DAMAGED AND REBODIED BY NC. AS 'C'

3] 390B, 391B, 392B, 395B, 405B, 407B, 409B, 451B, 766B, 784B, 786B, 790B, 794B, 799B, 801B, 804B, 808B –

4] 97C, 98C, 385C, 389C, 396C, 397C, 402C, 415C, 419C

5] 99, 386, 387, 394, 398, 418, 428, 435, 448, 787, 791, 812 –

6] 412B, 470B, 993B, 1001B, 1007B, 1385B, 1543B, 1545B – –

7] 430C, 578C, 602C, 623C, 626C, 629C, 633C, 635C, 641C, 643C

Notes

1   In Fog
2   In Works

Left:
'N1' No 1570 leaves the stop at Childs Hill on route 645.
Michael Rooum

TABLE 4 LIST OF TROLLEYBUSES DESTROYED OR REBODIED

NEW FLEET NO	ORIGINAL CLASS	DATE DAMAGED/ DESTROYED	DEPOT TO WHICH ALLOCATED WHEN DAMAGED/DESTROYED	IF DESTROYED	REBODIED BY		
					WEYMANN IN	EAST LANCS IN	NCB IN
95A	B2	07/11/40	BX	–	4/42	–	–
97C	B2	29/06/44	BX	–	–	–	2/46
98C	B2	29/06/44	BX	–	–	–	3/46
99~	B2	29/06/44	BX	DESTROYED	–	–	–
107A	B2	27/09/40	HT	–	4/42	–	–
364~	C3	30/07/44	WH WORKS	DESTROYED	–	–	–
385C	D2	29/06/44	BX	–	–	–	1/46
386~	D2	29/06/44	BX	DESTROYED	–	–	–
387~	D2	29/06/44	BX	DESTROYED	–	–	–
389C	D2	29/06/44	BX	–	–	–	2/46
390B	D2	29/06/44	BX	–	–	10/45	–
391B	D2	29/06/44	BX	–	–	9/45	–
392B	D2	29/06/44	BX	–	–	11/45	–
394~	D2	29/06/44	BX	DESTROYED	–	–	–
395B	D2	29/06/44	BX	–	–	4/46	–
396C	D2	29/06/44	BX	–	–	–	4/46
397C	D2	29/06/44	BX	–	–	–	1/46
398~	D2	29/06/44	BX	DESTROYED	–	–	–
402C	D2	29/06/44	BX	–	–	–	12/45
405B	D2	29/06/44	BX	–	–	3/46	–
406A	D2	07/11/40	BX	–	12/41	–	–
407B	D2	29/06/44	BX	–	–	12/45	–
409B	D2	29/06/44	BX	–	–	11/45	–
412B	D2	30/07/44	WH WORKS	–	–	3/46	–
415C	D2	29/06/44	BX	–	–	–	4/46
418~	D2	29/06/44	BX	DESTROYED	–	–	–
419C	D2	29/06/44	BX	–	–	–	8/46
428~	D2	29/06/44	BX	DESTROYED	–	–	–
430C	D2	30/07/44	WH WORKS	–	–	–	1/46
435~	D2	29/06/44	BX	DESTROYED	–	–	–
448~	D2	29/06/44	BX	DESTROYED	–	–	–
451B	D2	29/06/44	BX	–	–	3/46	–
470B	D2	30/07/44	WH WORKS	–	–	6/46	–
575C	E1	16/08/44	WW	–	–	–	5/46
578C	E1	30/07/44	WH WORKS	–	–	–	5/46
602C	E1	30/07/44	WH WORKS	–	–	–	5/46
621A	E2	09/03/41	WH	–	4/42	–	–
623C	E2	30/07/44	WH WORKS	–	–	–	5/46
626C	E2	30/07/44	WH WORKS	–	–	–	6/46
629C	E3	30/07/44	WH WORKS	–	–	–	9/46
633C	E3	30/07/44	WH WORKS	–	–	–	7/46
635C	E3	30/07/44	WH WORKS	–	–	–	6/46
641C	E3	30/07/44	WH WORKS	–	–	–	9/46
643C	E3	30/07/44	WH WORKS	–	–	–	9/46
766B	H1	29/06/44	BX	–	–	10/46	–
784B	H1	29/06/44	BX	–	–	2/47	–
786B	H1	29/06/44	BX	–	–	1/47	–
787~	H1	29/06/44	BX	DESTROYED	–	–	–
790B	H1	29/06/44	BX	–	–	8/46	–
791~	H1	29/06/44	BX	DESTROYED	–	–	–
792A	H1	07/11/40	BX	–	11/41	–	–
794B	H1	29/06/44	BX	–	–	4/47	–
795A	H1	07/11/40	BX	–	11/41	–	–
799B	H1	29/06/44	BX	–	–	1/47	–
801B	H1	29/06/44	BX	–	–	8/46	–
803A	H1	09/03/41	WH WORKS	–	3/42	–	–
804B	H1	29/06/44	BX	–	–	9/46	–
808B	H1	29/06/44	BX	–	–	1/47	–
812~	H1	29/06/44	BX	DESTROYED	–	–	–
861A	H1	13/10/40	WN	–	3/42	–	–
953~	M1	LATE 1943	WH	DESTROYED by fire in fog	–	–	–
993B	J2	30/07/44	WH WORKS	–	–	12/47	–
1001A	J2	13/10/40	HT	–	1/42	–	–
1001B	J2	30/07/44	WH WORKS	–	–	12/47	–
1007B	J2	30/07/44	WH WORKS	–	–	1/48	–
1123A	K1	08/11/40	SF	–	12/41	–	–
1128A	K1	18/09/40	SF	–	3/42	–	–
1244A	K2	11/10/40	CT	–	10/41	–	–
1247A	K2	09/03/41	WH WORKS	–	12/41	–	–
1285A	K1	11/10/40	WW	–	10/41	–	–
1365~	L1	11/11/42	HT	DESTROYED by fire in fog	–	–	–
1385B	L3	30/07/44	WH WORKS	–	–	1/48	–
1387~	L3	27/07/44	WW	DESTROYED	–	–	–
1492~	L3	09/03/41	WH WORKS	DESTROYED	–	–	–
1543B	M1	30/07/44	WH WORKS	–	–	4/48	–
1545B	M1	30/07/44	WH WORKS	–	–	3/48	–
1565A	N1	07/09/40	BW	–	6/42	–	–
1587A	N1	19/03/41	BW	–	2/42	–	–
Total; 78 – including 1001 twice					16	25	20